JENSON BUTTON

MY LIFE ON THE FORMULA ONE ROLLERCOASTER

www.**booksattransworld**.co.uk

For information on the Official Jenson Button Fan Club, contact:
Essentially Motorsport Limited, Equity Court,
73–75 Millbrook Road East, Southampton SO15 1RJ.
E-mail: info@jensonbutton.com

JENSON BUTTON

MY LIFE ON THE FORMULA ONE ROLLERCOASTER

JENSON BUTTON with DAVID TREMAYNE

BANTAM PRESS

LONDON · NEW YORK · TORONTO · SYDNEY · AUCKLAND

TRANSWORLD PUBLISHERS LTD
61–63 Uxbridge Road, London W5 5SA
a division of The Random House Group Ltd

RANDOM HOUSE AUSTRALIA (PTY) LTD
20 Alfred Street, Milsons Point, NSW 2061, Australia

RANDOM HOUSE NEW ZEALAND LTD
18 Poland Road, Glenfield, Auckland, New Zealand

RANDOM HOUSE SOUTH AFRICA (PTY) LTD
Endulini, 5a Jubilee Road, Parktown 2193, South Africa

Published 2002 by Bantam Press
a division of Transworld Publishers Ltd

A catalogue record for this book is available from the British Library.
ISBN 0593 04875X

Typeset in Goudy by Falcon Oast Graphic Art Ltd.
Printed in Great Britain by Clays Ltd, Bungay, Suffolk.

10 9 8 7 6 5 4 3 2 1

CONTENTS

FOREWORD

Sir Frank Williams

I first met Jenson Button in Barcelona in 1998 when he was introduced to me by a well-known journalist. Some while later, after the retirement of Alex Zanardi from our Grand Prix team, a number of Jenson's supporters, including many journalists, called to tell me that Jenson would make a natural and successful choice for a seat in the BMW Williams F1 team.

Circumstances saw Jenson given his opportunity and he rose to the occasion magnificently. He astonished both Patrick Head and myself with his total calmness and self-control, while in the second half of his first season he began consistently to outperform his team-mate.

As I write, Jenson has completed an extremely difficult year with Benetton Renault. I am sure many people have different views on why Jenson seemed to be submerged in various competitive difficulties and I can really offer no opinion on this matter. However, both Patrick and I recognize the talent that we saw first-hand in 2000 and know that this talent is not extinguishable. It is part of the man's spirit and part of his soul.

Regarding Jenson's future, as is the case with all Grand Prix drivers, it depends on his equipment and the efficiency of his team.
Youth is on his side and I personally believe that the Benetton
Renault team will deliver equipment of such calibre that Jenson
will be able comfortably to demonstrate his real potential.

My abiding memory of Jenson from 2000 was the fact that,
despite his instant fame and wealth – in England at least – he never
forgot his family and friends and they were frequently to be seen at
races enjoying the weekend with him. I was impressed.

ONE

DAD, I'M A FORMULA ONE DRIVER!

The moment I finally learned I was going to become a Formula One driver with Sir Frank Williams' team, I hugged my father and we both burst into tears. After weeks of uncertainty and the pressure of having to prove myself against a more experienced driver who was also in contention for the seat alongside Ralf Schumacher, the emotional release was just fantastic.

Dad and I barely had time to wipe our eyes before we were thrust through a door to face the world's media as BMW Williams made the announcement that I was to become Britain's latest, and youngest, Formula One recruit. The long uphill climb of the roller-coaster was over; now we had reached the first peak, the adrenalin-rush ride had begun. Just five days earlier I had celebrated my twentieth birthday.

How I became a member of the BMW Williams team is a long and complicated story. To get there I had a lot of help from some good people, all of whom shared a belief that I had the ability to back up their faith in me. I'd met journalist Joe Saward during my

Formula Ford days, at the Spanish Grand Prix in Barcelona in 1998 when I'd gone out with one of my former managers, Harald Huysman, to meet the Formula One team owners and have a look around. Joe knows Frank Williams very well, and I know that he put in not just one but several good words on my behalf. So did John Surtees, the only man ever to win World Championships on two wheels and four. He of course knew Frank from the old days. John had a meeting with him, then called my dad. 'Jenson will be getting a call, John,' he told him. I think Dad was a bit sceptical, but John was insistent. He was right. And towards the end of December 1999 I began to sense that things might be coming together. The news was out about a test I had done with Alain Prost's Formula One team in Barcelona earlier that month. It had gone very well; in particular, one of Alain's engineers, Humphrey Corbett, was saying a lot of complimentary things about me, which was really good of him.

I think it was a combination of all these inputs, allied to a land-slide of publicity material Keith Sutton of Sutton Motorsport Images had been sending out since my Formula Ford days, and approaches to Frank by my managers Harald and David Robertson, that finally persuaded Frank that it was at least worth taking a look.

Frank was facing a difficult situation at the time. Williams had an ongoing contract with Alex Zanardi. He had raced in Formula One with Lotus in the early 1990s before switching to America's single-seater ChampCar series and doing extremely well there. He was champion in 1997 and 1998, and Frank had signed him to a three-year contract which began in 1999. But Williams was struggling at that time and Zanardi had a disappointing season that year. In racing you are only as good as your last race, and Frank was wanting a divorce. I didn't know the full story, and in any case it was nothing to do with me, but Zanardi's return had coincided with

Williams' worst season for ages. It appeared that they were each looking for a way out.

It seemed obvious that if Zanardi were leaving, the Brazilian driver Bruno Junqueira, who was racing the Formula 3000 just one rung on the ladder beneath Formula One, was going to get the vacant drive. Junqueira was Williams' official test driver so everyone naturally assumed he was going to be the man for the 2000 season, especially when the French driver Olivier Panis decided to take a testing role with McLaren rather than move from an unhappy position with Prost into the second Williams seat.

I was out on my traditional Christmas booze-up with Trevor Carlin of Carlin Motorsport, Anthony 'Boyo' Hyatt and Martin Stone of AMT, friends from Formula Three. We were in the Atlantic Bar and Grill in London, on Friday, 18 December. The phone rings, and it was Dave Robbo [David Robertson]. 'My boy Jenson's been flying round Barcelona, testing for Prost. He's blowing everyone into the weeds.' Anthony spoke to him, then Trevor, then Trevor passed the phone over to me. Dave told me that Jenson had done a [1m] 24.4s. That was a good time. I'm pretty familiar with all the testing times we do, so I said he must have done that without any fuel in the car. Dave said, 'I'm telling you, he's got fifty kilos of fuel in it, same as Alesi had.' I didn't believe him. It was friendly banter.

The next day, I'd thought about it and I spoke to Frank. Obviously I knew our situation. Alex was going, so we were looking for someone. I mentioned it to Frank, on the Saturday of our works Christmas party. He said, 'Is there a question over the fifty kilos? How can we find out?' Well, Frank's son Jonathan is friends with Humphrey

Corbett, who was engineering Jenson in the Prost. So Johnnie got hold of Humphrey, who not only confirmed the fifty kilos but that he was on old tyres. And because of a clutch problem, the most sequential laps he'd had was eight. He said it was truly impressive. Frank and I spoke that night, and he said, 'All right, get him to contact me.' So I spoke with Harald Huysman on the Saturday. I told him, 'Don't get excited, don't keep ringing Frank, anything like that. You'll get nowhere. Frank wants to talk to Jenson, and I'll come back to you if there's any interest.'

I spoke again to Harald and David on the Sunday. Frank said he'd like to see Jenson. He called him, and asked him to come and see him. When Jenson and John came up I think Frank was quite impressed with Jenson's demeanour. He then phoned Dr Mario Thiessen and Gerhard Berger at BMW. Williams chooses its own drivers, but it was a question of courtesy since this was our first season with BMW. Frank told them that we were thinking of Jenson.

Jim Wright, Head of Marketing, Williams F1 team

Late in December, I got a call in my office in Oslo. 'Harald, this is Frank Williams. Can you take me through Jenson's test with Prost that we've been hearing about?' The test had missed the Christmas issues of the specialist magazines because of the way the pre-Christmas deadlines fell, but the word was already going around Formula One's gossip mill.

Harald Huysman, former joint manager

On Christmas Eve I was in the Vine Tree, a pub in Frome, my home town. I took my girlfriend Louise back there a few months ago because the place means quite a lot to me, with its nostalgically smelly sofa and sticky carpets! That night I was there with some old mates from school, seven or eight of us just having drinks the way you do around Christmas time. At one point my mobile rang and a husky voice on the other end said, 'Hello, Jenson, it's Frank Williams here.'

Well, it was Christmas Eve and I just figured it was another mate trying to wind me up. I said, 'Sorry, who are you?' And the husky voice said again: 'It's Frank Williams.' I still wasn't a believer, so I just said, 'What?' And he replied, still patient and now aware of my scepticism, 'No, no, really, it's Frank Williams.' I found out subsequently that Frank's assistant Hamish had called Keith Sutton to get my mobile phone number.

The situation became a little clearer to me at that point, and I just said to myself, 'Jeez!' It was so noisy in the pub I could barely hear myself think, so I ran outside, leaving my mates a bit shocked by my sudden erratic behaviour. It was freezing and I only had a T-shirt and jeans on, but it didn't matter. I couldn't feel the cold at all. I was talking to a man who had the power to transform my career. A man who could give me the thing I most wanted in my life.

The first thing Frank said was, 'I hope you don't think I'm not interested in your career just because I haven't phoned you yet,' which was nice of him. There were a number of teams I had already spoken to – not necessarily seriously, just chatting, the way you do to keep in contact. Williams had been one of them. Frank said he had been watching my progress and just wanted to get in touch to say he was interested and that he thought I'd done a good job.

He then asked me if I thought I was ready for Formula One. Well, how many times do you get asked that sort of question, by someone of Sir Frank Williams' stature? The footballing equivalent would be Sir Alex Ferguson asking some unknown teenager if he thought he was ready to play for Manchester United. I should have just said, 'Sure, Frank. When do you want me?' But my instinctive reaction was to be honest and say, 'No, I don't think I am right now. I've only driven an F1 car properly once, the Prost. I'm not sure about the starts.' After that we just talked as friends. We didn't really talk that much more about racing.

Jens's reaction was typically honest. He didn't stop to think about what Frank might have wanted to hear, he just said what he thought. There was Frank asking him if he was ready, and Jens was giving him reasons why he wasn't. And the things he was mentioning were silly little things!

Well, I'd heard what Frank was like, that he wasn't keen on managers and all that. So I rang him up myself. I told him I had been a bit worried myself that it might all be moving too fast too early, but that I'd had a word with Jenson and he seemed to think he was ready despite how hesitant he might have seemed on the phone. I told Frank that when I'd asked Jens the same question, he'd said to me, 'Dad, I'm ready. You have to trust me. With all that's going to happen now, you have to trust me. I'm telling you, I'm ready for Formula One.' I said to Frank, 'Frank, you don't know me yet but hopefully you will get to know me, if not now then later. I'm not lying to you now.' I explained to him what Jenson was like and why he'd said what he did. 'I'm not speaking for Jenson,' I said, 'but his answer was a totally honest answer. He thinks he's not ready for Formula One because he hasn't done any starts in Formula One yet. But that's just him.'

John Button

Frank invited me to go down to the factory at Grove, near Oxford, to see him, and Dad and I went there on 2 January 2000. During the course of our conversation Frank ran down a list of drivers who might be racing or testing with the team that year, and then he quite casually told me that I wasn't on it! In my head I was like, 'Oh! So why am I here?' He said they weren't sure what Zanardi was going to do; maybe he was going to stay; they would be deciding in the next couple of days. I was like, 'Oh!'

I had been getting all excited. I didn't know what to expect but I thought I'd at least be a test driver to start with. I didn't think I'd be racing, but you always hope. And then he came out with that. And he left it at that as well. He didn't put me out of my misery. I still don't know whether he'd decided a long time ago to give me a test and just didn't want to tell me and get me too excited and worked up about it. But I really wasn't sure what was going on as Dad and I left. We'd already turned down a five-year deal Ron Dennis at McLaren had offered me when I was in Formula Ford in 1998, and there were chances of test drives with Prost and Jaguar, who were talking about a race drive for 2001. But the team I was most interested in was BMW Williams. Now I wasn't sure what to think.

Subsequently I discovered that Alain Prost, who drove for Williams and won the World Championship with them in 1993, had spoken to Frank about the test I did for him. And then Frank had had a word with former Formula One driver Gerhard Berger, who was now the motorsport director at BMW, Williams' new engine supplier. When Frank asked me to go to Munich to meet Gerhard a few days after my visit to the factory at Grove, I began to think he might be interested in me after all, even though there had not yet been any suggestion of my testing a car for the team. I thought it was just a meeting, so Gerhard could see me and say hello. Obviously Dad and I were hoping for more, but that's all I really thought it was.

It was quite difficult for me to meet Gerhard for the first time, because I didn't know what to expect. He was a bit of a wild man to say the least in his racing days, and I'd been told so many stories about him, but he was pretty serious to begin with. I had two or three hours with him and didn't get a glimpse of the 'wild' side. He seemed a great bloke, and we got on really well. We went out for a meal and chatted about things, not just about racing. We just hit it off. Maybe he saw a lot of himself in me! I became his little project, I think.

Frank valued Gerhard's opinion, so Jenson was sent down to Munich to meet him. Gerhard liked him, and thought he had a good attitude. Our technical director, Patrick Head, was away in Brazil, so Frank decided, having spoken with Gerhard, that we were definitely going to test Jenson. But clearly he wanted to speak with Patrick first. Patrick wasn't quite sure, but said he would have a look at Jenson in Jerez. I think Frank probably had to work quite hard on Patrick initially, because Patrick thought we had some more fundamental problems to address at that time than giving a young guy a test – like getting the engine to run more than three laps.

Jim Wright, Head of Marketing, Williams F1 team

Within the week after Dad and I got back from Munich, Frank called me again. He didn't say anything about a race drive, he just said they wanted to test me. He didn't say for what reason. But that didn't matter. The invitation was exciting enough. In fact, I was elated. I had heard that Bruno Junqueira was also going to be testing at Jerez de la Frontera, the circuit in the middle of Spain's sherry-producing region that had hosted the Spanish GP on and off over the years, and I knew he'd done quite a bit of testing in the car already. I was looking forward to my opportunity, of course, but I knew in those circumstances that it would be very tough.

My introduction upset what was already a delicate political balance. Frank's partner, the team's technical director Patrick Head, has a reputation for not suffering fools gladly, and he has strong views on drivers just as he has strong views on most topics in Formula One. Patrick already felt that Junqueira was the most straightforward answer in terms of a replacement for Zanardi. He'd tested with the team for some time, he was quick and he was there. It was like he already had pole position for the drive. Patrick values year-on-year continuity very highly, especially when it comes to developing racing cars, and anyone could see that it made sense in some ways to slot the experienced test driver into the second seat because it would mean the whole operation could continue with minimal upheaval. My schooling might effectively have ended when I was fourteen or fifteen, but you didn't have to be a genius to figure out that giving a test to a rookie a couple of months before the new season opened was probably the last thing Patrick needed right then. The new alliance between Williams and BMW was having a troubled baptism thanks to the fragility of its new engines, and nobody needed to start worrying about babying along a new boy no-one knew. Junqueira knew everybody on the team and had done a lot of kilometres of running, and could slot right in.

I was already familiar with Jerez after spending two days there the previous December testing with the SuperNova and Fortec F3000 teams, but still, I was very nervous about the test. When Dad and I turned up on 13 January, a Thursday, it was wet. Of course I had it in the back of my mind that I really needed to impress Frank and

Patrick, but you put those things out of your immediate thoughts when you're driving. I was concentrating so much on being as quick as I could and doing the best I could for the team that I was barely aware of who was around me in the garage. Later I would read or hear things about how I'd been so cool and calm, but people sometimes see a very different thing from the reality!

Williams had brought along an interim car for us to drive, the FW21B, a 1999 model fitted with the BMW engine in place of the Supertec unit it had raced with the previous year. The first track day dawned warm and sunny, and there were a lot of quick guys there. McLaren had David Coulthard and test driver Olivier Panis; Jaguar had Johnny Herbert, Eddie Irvine and my old Formula Three sparring partner Luciano Burti; Sauber Petronas and BAR Honda were there too. But in the end it was an anti-climax for Bruno and me: he suffered a transmission problem in the morning, I had engine trouble in the afternoon. Neither of us got a flying lap.

The following morning the track was damp but not wet enough to fit the car with Michelin's specially patterned rain tyres, so out I went on the usual grooved dry-weather rubber. Although I was apprehensive, I wasn't as nervous as I might have been. Looking back, I appreciate of course how that test changed my fortunes, but at the time I didn't see it that way. I just thought it was a test, and I just wanted to drive a Formula One car and show what I could do. So I wasn't as nervous as I should have been and most people would have been.

To the layman, putting himself into my driving boots, that probably seems unlikely, to say the least. Everyone who dreams of these things imagines how they'd feel, without knowing what a Formula One car feels like. But talk to most racing drivers and they will tell you the same thing: all you are focused on when you're in the car is getting the job done. What you have to remember is that since the age of eight I had been driving racing machines. Sure, the 800bhp BMW Williams FW21B was an awfully long way removed from my first drive, a 5bhp Cadet kart back in 1988. But over the years I'd done this sort of thing many times. Every rung up the racing ladder is a new adventure, but each rung is relative. I'd moved from the Cadet to a 16bhp 100cc Junior TKM kart, and on to a 20bhp JICA, 26bhp ICA and 30bhp Formula A and Formula Super A karts. Then I'd climbed into a 140bhp Formula Ford single-seater racing car, followed by a 220bhp Formula Three and a 500bhp Formula 3000. I'd also driven my first Formula One cars for McLaren and Prost at the end of the previous year.

Obviously going from any other formula racing car to a Formula One car is still the biggest step you'll ever make, but it was just a mega feeling the first time I left the pits. The thing I was worried about most was pulling out of the pits. I really didn't want to stall it, especially as on my first time I'd done just that, embarrassing myself in front of everyone. It was the first time I'd used a hand clutch. I knew when I got on the circuit it would be OK, though.

Once I got on the track it was a bit scary, but driving in damp conditions that first time out with BMW Williams was possibly the best thing that could have happened. Had it been straight out for a flying lap in the dry, I think that would have been tough. The braking is so much later and harder in the dry and you're carrying so many 'g's in the high-speed corners. As it was, I was saved by engine trouble from that fate, and the rain the next day handed me the best conditions in which to acclimatize to the car.

In my head, for sure, ran this mantra that I mustn't screw up. Definitely that was there. But then again, you want to push to the limit to show you can be quick from the first lap. You don't want to make a mistake, but you do want to push like hell so they can see you're on it straight away. I made a conscious effort to look as good as I could from the outset. I did some routine installation laps to check that everything was working properly, then I did my first three flying laps. I felt completely confident and in control of the situation, and I really, really enjoyed myself. I just couldn't stop laughing at the sheer power at my disposal on the straights. It was just awesome! The track was greasy because of the damp, so I could drive the car on the throttle as well as the steering. I suppose the feeling is similar to what tightrope walkers experience, that exhilaration of juggling speed and balance and walking a thin line without ever overstepping it. I had a ball. The BMW Williams was a beautiful car to drive, although, like any racing car, it wasn't easy to handle on the limit. But it was what I had waited for for so long, and I felt completely relaxed and at home. My best lap was 1m 25.75s, which people seemed pleased about.

When I came in after those first few flying laps, I caught sight of Harald just shaking his head. He'd been a mad racer himself, but he couldn't believe what he'd seen.

The first time Jenson passed by I was at the back of the pits, near the fast right-hander where Martin Donnelly had his big crash in 1990. It was half wet, half dry, very difficult conditions. I will never forget it. Jenson came by with the engine just singing, Waaaaa! Waaaaa! Waaaaa!, as he changed gears. He was going flat out. I was so taken aback that I spilled my coffee! I turned to my partner, David Robertson, who was with me and who shared my hopes for Jenson's future, and said, 'That's it. I'm not watching any more.' I've been a maniac on the track in my time, racing in Formula Three in Europe and Formula Atlantic in America, but I just couldn't bear to watch the rest of his first laps. I just thought he was gonna stuff it, but of course he didn't. He was brilliant.

Harald Huysman

The only problems I had on that first test were with the varying conditions and the fact that the car never wanted to run for long. The track would dry a bit, then get wet again, then begin to dry again, and the car would keep stopping at inconvenient moments. From the team's point of view it was all pretty inconclusive. It was very hard to make valid comparisons between drivers' lap times when track conditions were changing all the time and the car's reliability was unpredictable. It was pretty trying for me too. I was hoping for a quick decision; instead, I found everything being drawn out because nobody felt able to form any kind of conclusion – not all that surprising when you consider the investment any Formula One team makes these days. It costs millions of dollars to design and develop a car, and millions more to design and develop its engine. Then you have to throw more millions at running it in the seventeen-race World Championship. A team of BMW Williams' calibre would easily invest $200 million during the course of a season. So neither Frank nor Patrick was going to make a snap decision on a second driver when the stakes were that high.

Frank was the main driver behind our decision to give Jenson a test opportunity. I thought with our first year with BMW that we would have quite enough problems on our plate. I was quite committed to the idea of running Bruno Junqueira in the second car. He seemed to have a good brain and be pretty quick and I was quite happy with that because I thought we'd have bigger problems on our plate.

Then I saw that Prost had run Jenson and that he'd gone pretty well at Barcelona. But I didn't really think too much about it. I was in Brazil over Christmas and New Year and Frank rang me up down there and said he wanted to give Jenson a run and then make a decision

after that test. And I said something to the effect that I thought that would limit the mileage by splitting it between Bruno and Jenson and that meant that if we *were* going to choose Bruno then he would have less mileage under his belt. But I was happy to go along with it.

By the time I'd seen Jenson do his third lap at Jerez, I thought, 'Goodness me, this chap is pretty good.'

In fact we were having all sorts of installation problems at that time with the E41 BMW V10 engine. It was running perfectly well on the dyno [the dynamometer, a piece of static equipment onto which the engine is bolted to assess performance], but in the interim car it was having problems so we didn't get very much mileage at all in Jerez. So we decided to leave it and repeat the test between Bruno and Jenson in Barcelona.

Patrick Head, Technical Director, Williams F1 team

As the second January test session, in Barcelona, drew near, I realized that things were dragging on a lot longer than usual, that normally they would have picked someone by this stage. Seeing how Bruno had so much more experience than me, I was still assuming they'd go straight for him. In the end, I think BMW Williams' decision to give me another test wasn't based on what I had done over the three days we were in Jerez, but purely on those first three flying laps I did when the track was really slippery. David Coulthard and other quick guys were out at the same time and I was running at a similar speed. I showed I could get on it quickly, and I think that's what swung things in my favour for another shot. (I discovered later that the mechanics were all getting quite excited about my speed, that Patrick had told them all to calm down and not show any emotion when I came back into the pits!)

So when I headed out to Spain I figured that things were still up in the air. I thought to myself, 'Hang on a sec. There's nobody in the driving seat for the racing yet, Zanardi's left, and Bruno and I are the only two geezers that have driven the car in the last two months! This must be it!' Nobody put it into words for us, but while we were travelling on flights backwards and forwards Dad and I put it together like that.

I went out to that test in Barcelona in a new frame of mind, because this was no longer just about a possible test drive. I knew this could mean me racing in Formula One in 2000. Williams still might try me and reject me, and other Formula One teams might think I wasn't worth worrying about after that, but to be honest that didn't concern me. We thought it would be positive even if I didn't get it, that people would put any rejection down to my lack of experience rather than anything else. I just knew that what I did on the track on Sunday, 23 January, the day before BMW Williams was scheduled to announce to the world its package for 2000, was going to decide the path my career would follow over the next few years.

Motor racing history is littered with the names of quick racing drivers who had their moment in the spotlight and then faded, and I knew that three quick flying laps on a damp track in Jerez were only going to be a talking point for a finite time. In Formula One the pressure is on you to perform every time you go out in the car. There are never any easy rides. You either do it or you don't. It was effectively a straight shoot-out between Bruno and me; one of us was going to go home a very disappointed young man. I was determined it wasn't going to be me. That might sound callous, but when you encapsulate just what motor racing means, it comes down to precisely that, whether you're fighting for a drive or a victory. It's you or them.

Again, although I was super-aware of the pressure hovering in the background, I've always been an optimistic person by nature and I've always looked ahead. I handle pressure well, probably because although I'm very focused I'm also a pretty laid-back character. I just didn't have any time for morbid thoughts about what I would do if I didn't come out on top. I guess I'm fortunate like that. I just don't dwell on negative things, and I think that's a major help in a sport as competitive as ours. You have to have maximum self-confidence and self-belief. Team owners are a bit like animals: they can sense when you're afraid of them. They have this ability to spot drivers who don't believe in themselves. And they need to have it. You aren't going to jeopardize your chances by backing a guy who doesn't have the right mentality. All of us out there believe we can be the best. If we didn't think that, we'd never have got this far.

By the time the test got under way, again with the interim FW21B car, it was already clear that BMW had made some impressive progress on reliability with its latest engines. Both Bruno and I were able to get plenty of running. It was warm and sunny, though the ambient temperature never got above 14°C. We'd been told that the contest would be decided in the main by sheer pace, but I knew that wouldn't be everything.

Bruno ran in the morning, which meant that I had to hang around while he got to have all the fun. In two stints he did twenty-six laps, with a fastest time of 1m 23.5s. That was pretty quick, good enough for fourteenth place on the grid for the 1999 Spanish GP there. When I'd driven the Prost at the track the previous December, my best had been 1m 24.4s. Food for thought.

I got my run in the afternoon, in similar weather conditions. I did twenty-one laps in two stints, and my fastest time was 1m 23.34s. I was faster than Bruno, and I was elated. The difference between us was pretty small, but it was bigger if you added up the times over the complete lap distances. I began to feel cautiously hopeful, but I still couldn't be sure if I had done enough. I had no idea, after all, what Frank and Patrick were really looking for. All I knew was that I had done my best. Now came the agony of waiting to find out whether that had been good enough.

When it came to the mechanical side of things, the setting up of the car, I was nowhere near as good as Bruno. He had far more experience than me in that area. The team made us do a sort of written test to show what we knew about that aspect of a Formula One car. It was like being back at school – pretty scary! I know I didn't do anything like as well as Bruno on that test. I knew it almost as soon as we'd finished it. But not only was I faster, I felt I had been more consistent on the track – even though I found it very difficult physically because I hadn't done a huge number of laps in a Formula One car – and I knew Frank and Patrick liked that.

By now it was well into January and we were committed to launching the new car on the 24th and to announcing our Compaq principal sponsorship that day. The run-off kept getting put off, but BMW found a temporary solution and wanted to test on the 23rd. They thought they could do enough to give us sufficient laps.

Bruno went first and did a 1m 23.5s, a good time, and he came in and was pretty pleased with that. I think he did two 23.5s. Then it was Jenson's turn and it was getting pretty late in the day, about four o'clock, light beginning to go and all of that. He went out and in ten or twelve laps did a 23.3s and looked very accomplished. Maybe Jenson's times were all accomplished in less time, but in fairness, because Bruno went earlier and the circuit

had been slightly damp, that probably would explain the difference. Clearly we would have known that, so it wouldn't have been a factor.

Frank and Patrick looked through the data and had meetings with the engineers to ask what their opinions were. Frank called me at eleven o'clock that night and said, 'Jim, I know you want me to make the decision on the driver tomorrow, but I can't do it. I just haven't seen enough of them. They are very evenly matched, but for the sake of a few days I'm not prepared to make that decision.'

Okay, I understood that. It wasn't a huge problem. We told Compaq, BMW and the BBC's Steve Rider, who was going to be master of ceremonies for the whole thing, and what we agreed to do was present both of the drivers alongside Ralf and say it was incredibly close and that we needed more time to evaluate them. They were both doing a fantastic job.

Jim Wright

Basically, when I turned in that Sunday night I really didn't have a clue what the decision was going to be. I figured the team would be heavily behind Bruno on the technical side, but really it was just too confusing to try to work it out. When I got to the circuit on Monday morning, the day of the launch, I was still none the wiser. I could see people in the team smiling, and it was like, 'Would they be smiling at me if I hadn't got it, or are they smiling out of sympathy?' It was a really difficult situation. Harald was flying around like a lunatic trying to find out if I'd won or not, asking everyone and getting nowhere. None of us would know before Frank finally told me.

Bruno and I, dressed in our racing gear, had both had photos taken that morning ready for the press pack, because one of us would be the second race driver and the other the test driver. The decision was due to be announced publicly one way or another around eleven o'clock. Just after ten-thirty I got pulled out of the garage by Nav Sidhu, who worked on the public relations side for Williams (he's now with Jaguar, and as 2000 progressed we would become quite close mates). He said, 'Frank wants to have a word.' This was it. I immediately thought, 'Did Bruno go up before me? Or is he going up after me?' I found out that he'd gone before me, which I felt just made things even worse. I thought that meant he'd got it and I hadn't.

Nav and I waited in this little room at the circuit, a tiny room just big enough for both of us, really. Nav was smiling at me. I imagined he wouldn't be smiling if I hadn't landed the drive. Of course I'd assumed that he knew; it turned out that he didn't. Then Bruno came out of another room and Nav told me to go in. Bruno didn't say anything, but he didn't look that upset either. He certainly wasn't smiling, though.

I walked in and knelt down next to Frank. 'Jenson,' he began, 'obviously we have seen you drive in the last test and we have come to a conclusion that you will be driving with us next year alongside Ralf.' I thought, 'Oh my God!' There was no reaction from Frank. Just a little smile. Then Ralf came in, and I remember it so clearly, it's unbelievable. I shook his hand and Frank said to him, 'Did you hear?' And Ralf said, 'Yeah, I knew it ages ago that Jenson had it.' And then he started talking about not being picked up from his hotel that morning. No-one had turned up for him. I just stood there watching them argue. It was the weirdest thing. I thought, 'Hmm, maybe this isn't such a good thing.' Later, I found out that the verdict had been for Bruno on the Sunday night because he was as quick and his technical knowledge was better, but then it changed in my favour on Monday.

After a short while Frank said to me, 'Go on, go and tell your father.' So Dad was brought into the room just as Frank was leaving, and that was when I told him.

'Dad, I'm a Formula One driver!'

He just burst into tears and hugged me, and I burst into tears big time too. It was really strange. There we were in this little room in the old paddock suite at the circuit in Barcelona, the world's journalists waiting impatiently outside, two men hugging and crying. Then Dad and I found Harald and David. I told them too and they burst into tears as well. Then I phoned home to tell the rest of my family. Mum was out. She told me later she had only popped down to the shop for fifteen minutes. When she got back she heard the tearful message I'd left. She told me she'd bawled her eyes out too. It was quite emotional – the most emotional I think I've ever been.

I listened in to the drivers' radio communications during the shoot-out. Jens was talking as he came down the pit lane on his in-lap and his voice was crystal clear, low tone, relaxed. Junqueira sounded out of breath, excited, much less relaxed. So I think all of that counted too.

I think Frank was still in a quandary as to which driver to choose. When he was driving into the circuit on Monday morning – the day the team would officially unveil both its new car and its new driver to the media – Patrick called him on his mobile and said, 'Frank, have you made a decision?' And Frank said, 'No.' Patrick said, 'Well, I think we've got to. And I think we go with Button.' There was a bit of a pause, then Frank said, 'Yeah, I agree. Let's do it.'

Looking back, that was staggering. The world's press was going ape-shit. We hadn't even done anything!

When it had happened for Damon Hill with Frank back in 1993, everyone at least knew Damon and he had done a couple of Grand Prix races and loads of testing for the team, and had raced in F3000 for two years. Everyone knew what he could do. Hardly anyone in Formula One really had any idea about Jens. Only a couple of guys knew what he'd done in karting and then Formula Ford and Formula Three. And if the majority of these people didn't know Jens, they certainly didn't know me. Yet within minutes it seemed like everyone in the world's media was my mate! It was a crazy situation.

I've never been in awe of anyone, never asked for anyone's autograph, or anything like that. There are people I respect, in my chosen sport of motor racing. I'd known Bernie Ecclestone years ago, and knew of Frank and Patrick. It was difficult to begin with, because I felt a bit uncomfortable with them early on because of who they are, but I wasn't in awe of any of them. It was just business as usual. I think that was a bonus for us. There was no bowing or scraping, though I had a lot of respect for them. I was really thinking, 'How soon can I start talking to them the way I speak to everyone else?' Well, two swear words, and shortly after that Frank was relaxed too. Patrick as well, in our little private bit of the garage. It was quite funny. But to begin with I didn't know these people and I was very wary of Frank, obviously, with the press around. Frightened to death of Patrick.

We'd been told a decision wouldn't be made until the afternoon. The launch was in the morning, around ten o'clock initially. But it got delayed. And then a guy came up and said, 'Oh, Mr Button, will you come with me?' I was stood with some press people and my first thought was, 'What have I done?' That's just what I thought! 'What have I done wrong? Maybe they don't like me speaking to the press . . .'

They took me off and stuck me in this room. It was like being outside the headmaster's office. Then this guy walked in, and I saw Frank. And that was it. I thought, 'What does he want with me?' And then Jens walked towards me and I said, 'What's happening?' Jens replied, 'Shall we tell him?' I said, 'What? What?' It just didn't click. Jens just smiled at me and said those immortal words: 'Dad, I'm a Formula One driver!' He put his arms round me and we hugged, and then we both burst into bloody tears! It was incredible. One of the great moments in both our lives. Everything felt so wonderful.

They took us straight away to meet the press, and suddenly I was treated like royalty. I kept thinking, 'That's my little man there!' I felt so proud as I was pushed down to the front with Jens. Nobody wanted to go and see the car. They all just wanted to talk to Jens, and I gave out the little titbits about running out of money once in karting and having to borrow it so we could get back home from a circuit in Scotland, that sort of thing.

That day, I don't know where it went. I can't remember the evening, except for Jens saying to me, 'How about going for dinner with a Formula One driver tonight, Dad?' That brought some reality to the situation. I sat across the table and looked at him and thought, 'You're a Formula One driver, but you're still my son.' It still felt the same. Really weird.

John Button

We were due to kick off at eleven. Frank rang me with twenty minutes to go. 'Jimmy boy, I'm in the car on the way in, just spoken with Patrick. We've agreed to go with Jenson. We've talked it through. We're going with Jenson. Can you arrange things? But before anything is said, I want to see Bruno.'

I think ultimately they decided that the two of them were very, very close, but that it was worth a gamble on going with Jenson because they felt that of the two he had less experience of driving at that sort of speed and therefore had greater potential. Bruno did have a fair bit more experience at that stage. I was very surprised, given Frank's comments twelve hours earlier, but I was very pleased because we had a spectacular launch which made the front pages of every UK newspaper. It was *News at Ten* stuff. The relationship with Compaq could not have kicked off in a better way. People will say it was staged, but those are the facts. It just happened that way. And it was a fantastic story.

You know, the one thing that struck me most about Jenson in the heat of all the hoop-la: here was a young guy going for a Formula One drive, just turned twenty, and when he came into the pits after the run-off he came blasting in, knew where the white speed-limit line was, braked hard and got the car on the speed limiter right by the white line. And I thought, 'This is a guy who's got the spare capacity to be able to look at that kind of detail and apply himself to it. He's either doing it almost sub-consciously, because he knows that's what's expected of a Formula One driver, or he's doing it to impress.' Anyway, I reported that back to Frank and Patrick and our engineers, for what it was worth. I'm sure it wasn't part of the consideration, but just as an observer watching from the outside I was really impressed with that. He was just really cool. That word is used far too often these days, but he was cool. It wasn't that he didn't want it – he

was desperate for it. But he was cool. Even on the Monday morning, when it was likely there wasn't going to be a decision and he'd been told that, he was resigned, courteous and professional. The other nice touch was that before he went on to the stage once a decision had been made, he went and shook Bruno's hand. Bruno was distraught, he really was.

It was a privilege to watch the events unfold. It really was. It was quite an amazing sequence. And totally unstaged. It just happened that way. We were lucky. It worked out very well.

Jim Wright

After all the decisions had finally been revealed, I just felt really nervous. Not because of the driving but because of all the media people I then had to go and face. While all the tense revelations were being made behind the scenes, Steve Rider was on the other side of the door and the press conference was already well under way. I felt terrified at the prospect of speaking in front of loads of people I didn't know, but also because I'd have to sit next to Bruno. I didn't get a chance to say anything to him before we got pitched into the media launch, just to shake hands. The funny thing is, when we had talked together we had never talked about the drive, it was always about other things. We were very friendly towards each other, but we just didn't discuss the racing side. It was a potentially difficult situation, but I think we both handled it very well.

After the launch we spoke, and I just told him it was really hard to know what to say. He was very good. He just said, 'No, no problem. I still have another year in Formula 3000. This was a chance to get into Formula One, but there'll be other chances.' He was fantastic about it. I admired him a lot for that. He went on to win the F3000 Championship that year and to get a ride in the American ChampCars single-seater series, and he won the Road America race in 2001, so he didn't do too badly out of it either.

I started work as a Formula One race driver straight away. The Tuesday morning after the announcement was surreal. As I went out on my installation lap, just to warm the car up and check that everything was working properly, the surrounding countryside was covered in a blanket of snow. No-one got the photo of me coming back down the pit lane smothered in all this white stuff on my first run as a pukka BMW Williams team member. It would have been a mega-shot. And because they couldn't start running straight away as it began to snow again, everyone started making snowmen! It was a weird way to start my real Formula One career.

Later that day, when the snow had melted, Panis set the fastest time on a wet track. The Saubers were next. I revelled in my first experience of driving the Williams FW21B in the wet, and lapped in 1m 35.89s, fractions ahead of Ralf in the new car. I hoped that was going to be a good omen.

TWO

SCHOOLBOY RACER

Where did I get the name Jenson? That's what everyone always wants to know. Well, Dad used to race in rallycross against a guy called Erling Jensen. Dad loved the sound of his surname, and Mum agreed it was a cool name to go with Button. But Erling's name was spelled 'en'; they changed it to 'on' so people wouldn't think I was named after the Jensen sports car. They still do, though.

I was born in Frome, Somerset, on 19 January 1980, the year Alan Jones went on to win the World Championship with Frank Williams and Patrick Head. I'm the baby of the family, with three older sisters: Natasha, Samantha and Tanya. At school I had all sorts of nicknames, among them Zipper and Jennifer, which I could figure out. But another was Genitals, and I'm really not sure where that one came from.

Mum and Dad say I was a good kid, but I was hyperactive and strong-minded from a very early age. A little bit mischievous with my sisters, which is normal. I watched motorsport on television from an early age and used to study it closely. When I was five or six I'd point out to Dad when one car was getting ready to pass another. Realizing in precisely which direction my youthful passions lay, for my seventh birthday Dad bought me a Yamaha 50cc scrambling bike. I had it on display at a hall we hired for my party. I wanted to show it off to all my school friends, so I did a display driving round the hall. The bike was quite heavily restricted, but I guess that was my first public appearance. Later, after half an hour driving round the green outside our house, I told Dad I was bored. It wasn't quick enough. So he took the restrictor off. I jumped back on, cranked the throttle wide open and up came the front wheel. I fell straight off the back.

Dad used to take me to Longleat so I could ride it on tracks round there, but I got fed up with that too after a while. There was a scrambling track near Bridgewater, so he took me there, and I was soon getting quicker and quicker, sliding the back out and sticking out my foot round corners. I was having a ball, but he was worried because some of the older kids were crashing. He told me to stay cool.

Just before Christmas that year, 1987, Dad and Mum separated. They decided it was the best thing. That meant that for a while I saw Dad only at weekends. I was still hyperactive, so he'd take me to the seaside or to funfairs. It always seemed to be cold and wet. I'd decided that I wanted a bigger motorbike, an 80cc, but he wasn't at all impressed with that idea.

Then he went to the Racing Car Show at Earls Court and bumped into an old friend, Keith Ripp, the accessory magnate. Dad mentioned the problems he was having keeping me occupied. Keith suggested this kart that he had hanging up on the Rippspeed stand. It was for a new category called Cadets, for kids eight to twelve years old. Dad wasn't interested in any of that; what he liked the sound of was the fact that it had four wheels. He wrote Keith a cheque there and then.

Early on Christmas Day Dad dragged me out of the house, still in my pyjamas, and there it was! It was a Zip with a 60cc 5bhp Comer engine, but I wasn't bothered about the details. I just leapt on and started shouting for him to start it up. Dad was living on a farm at that time, so off I went down the drive, along a small side road and into a pub car park. I nearly lost control and hit a parked car, which almost gave him a heart attack, so on Boxing Day he took me down to a disused airport at Bridgewater. That was much better. But after twenty minutes, typically, I was back telling him that I was bored. So he found a phone box and called the only kart track he'd ever heard of – Clay Pigeon in Dorset. It was open.

When we got there my eyes popped out. It was a proper, honest-to-God race track. It was wet and we only had slick tyres, but Dad didn't buy any wets because he thought I'd have more fun sliding the kart around on the slicks. He was right! We made a lot of trips to Clay Pigeon. Dad taught me about racing lines, braking, smoothness. He did the classic thing of standing at my normal braking point and then slowly, lap by lap, taking a step closer to the corner so that I had to brake later. Inevitably he soon went one step too far and I slid straight off.

Eventually, club members began asking us when we were going to start racing. Dad said no, we weren't going to do that, it was just something to do at weekends. But one day we were testing and the favourite for the championship, Matthew Davies, was there testing with his father. We'd read about Matt. I used to sit on his bumper, lap after lap. That set Dad thinking. I knew what I wanted to do, and eventually he gave in and asked me if I wanted to race. My answer was immediate: yes!

My first race was at Clay Pigeon in May 1988; I was eight years and four months old. It was wet, and I remember at one stage I could only just see Dad. He was standing on the track frantically waving at me to slow down. He had a great attitude: he just told me to relax and enjoy myself. That's what we were there for. Somebody wrote a lot later in my career that I passed thirty-four karts to win that day, but there weren't that many karts in the race. But I did have to start at the back because I was a novice, and I did pass all the karts that were out there, and I did win. The feeling was fantastic. First kart race, first win. At the finish Dad ran onto the track and was jumping up and down, like he was Team Lotus boss Colin Chapman. I was pretty pleased with myself too.

That night I slept with the little trophy I won.

After that Dad asked me if I wanted just to do club racing, or whether I wanted to take it seriously. He let me have a think about it, but again I already knew. I wanted to do it seriously. He told me some of the fun would go and that it would be harder work, but that was OK by me. Matt's father suggested that we test at tracks where other championship races would be held, that I could learn from Matt – which was great of him. So that's what we did. And it *was* hard work, especially for Dad, who was paying for it all.

That first season I raced again at Clay, as well as Dunkerswell in Devon and Little Rissington in Gloucester. It was terrific fun, and I ended up winning the club championship at Clay Pigeon.

Matt moved into Juniors for 1989, so we bought his Gillard kart and quite a bit of his equipment and engines. But it wasn't only on the track that I was taking a step in a different direction. Mum remarried that year and moved away to where her new husband was living; it was decided that the best thing for me would be to move in with Dad, along with two of my sisters. He had a new partner called Pippa, so she would be helping him to bring us up. Not long after that we moved to a new place in Vobster, a small hamlet outside Frome.

In 1989 I finished second in the Cadet Championships and won the Super Prix at Silverstone. But the biggest race of the lot was a televised event called the Clay Pigeon Super Prix. I won that by a huge margin against guys like Daniel Wheldon, Marc Hynes, Justin Wilson, Anthony Davidson, Craig Murray, all of whom I would get to race against much higher up the motorsport ladder in the years to come. Benetton Formula One driver Johnny Herbert was there to present the award at the end of the evening. Apparently, one of the commentators had said on my last lap, 'Do you think this kid will get to Formula One? Are we looking at a new Johnny Herbert?'

Dad was always cautious when anyone asked things like that, but the truth is that we were already planning to get to Formula One. We talked about it a lot, and we looked at all the reasons why other drivers who had shown promise in karting didn't get through to Formula One. There were so many reasons, and often one of them was the fathers themselves. They just didn't train the drivers in the right way.

One of the things Dad used to get me to do was watch successful drivers being interviewed on television, to see how they came over – whether they were telling the truth, that sort of thing. Later, I did it with other sports people. One day, when I was lounging on the floor, head propped up on my arms, a politician was speaking on the TV. I just turned to Dad and said, 'That guy is lying.'

We had a good season in 1990, driving a Wright kart. We had a lot of help at that stage from British champion Simon Wright, who made the karts, and Dad was now preparing my engines (he had a fair amount of experience in that department: in his rallycross days he had driven a Volkswagen Beetle; one of his rivals, Franz Wurz, the father of Alex against whom I would later race in Formula One, also had a Beetle, but his had been built for him by Porsche whereas Dad had built his own). But Dad and I were going through a difficult patch at the time and he found it hard to persuade me that getting the last bit out of the kart was down to me. We had a very good relationship and I think he was afraid of putting its closeness in jeopardy. So he tried not to argue with me.

There was a race in November that year at Rye House in Hertfordshire, and we were helped there by a friend of Simon's, Dave Spence, who had lots of experience in karting himself and through his son Jamie, who also raced. We stayed at their house and watched videos Dad had taken during the day's practice. We went through them very carefully. Dave explained to me what I was doing wrong. That was my first experience of examining my racing closely. The next day I was really quick, so the analysis did pay off. Dave and I really seemed to click that year. It was one of those magic relationships. Jamie often came along too, to offer advice. It was a fantastic time.

In 1990 I finished third in the series and in 1991 I was the British Cadet champion. I have really fond memories of those days, when I was nine going on ten and racing against good drivers such as Daniel Wheldon, Anthony Davidson and Tom Sisley. I raced Daniel again in Formula Ford, Anthony is making his name in Formula Three, and Tom has won races in Formula Renault. I get a real kick out of seeing their careers progress. Racing them was so competitive, it's unbelievable. Such good racing. I still look back on that time and think, 'Wow, those were some of the best years of my life. Really, really good fun.' It was really competitive, but you were friends with them all. I was never really much of a fan of other sports. I used to do a bit of track and field at school, mainly long-distance running rather than the short stuff, maybe a bit of swimming, but never cricket. And the only time I had for football was at races, when we'd all have a kick-about together and then get in our karts and race each other on the circuit. Wonderful, carefree days.

The year 1991 was particularly great. I knew it would be my last year in Cadets. We stayed with Simon's karts, and Dad's engine preparation business was now doing quite nicely because of the success we had enjoyed. I won all five rounds of the British Championship in which I competed, and the O Plate Championship at the end of the year. I won every race I entered, but it was an expensive season. We were up in Scotland at one point, at the Larkhall kart track, and, unknown to me, Dad had maxed his credit card and run out of cash, so he had to borrow the money from Simon for the fuel to get us home. That was how tight things were.

Our success left us with a sour taste in the mouth, however. My speed, and the fact that Dad was preparing my engines, led to accusations that we must be cheating. Dad spoke to the RAC MSA, the governing body of the sport in the UK. We took our engines there so they could be stripped, inspected and sealed. After each race they had to go back to the RAC to ensure that the seals hadn't been broken. That quietened things down for bit, until somebody suggested that Dad had the RAC MSA in his pocket!

At the final round at Rowrah in the Lake District the atmosphere was getting to everyone. Jens won and was pulled in, together with the other drivers in the top six. The other five karts were checked minutely, and the second-placed one was excluded for having an oversize carburettor. Then they came to our kart and there was almost a riot. Everyone wanted to see it being stripped down. The scrutineers had to push people out of the scrutineering hut. Things only quietened down when the Clerk of the Course threatened to disqualify everyone if they didn't back off.

Of course the engine was fine, and the scrutineers resealed it. One of the chief scrutineers said to me, 'They

should watch the way your son drives, rather than worrying so much about his engine.' Nevertheless, somebody still protested against the scrutineers' findings regarding the second-placed kart. That protest was eventually thrown out, but because of that Jens was the only driver to take home a trophy that night. We reckoned that was just deserts.

John Button

We rounded off the season, and my Cadet career, in October by winning the O Plate at Buckmore Park in Kent, where I had a fabulous dice with Tom Sisley, whose father Bill owns the track. Tom and I really enjoyed that scrap, passing and repassing each other. It was karting just as it should be: hard, but clean and fair.

As Cadet champion I was supposed to get my trophy at the end-of-season awards ceremony, but for some reason it was decided that Cadets would not be represented that year. So I never got to go up and get my bit of silver. But Dad knew somebody at *Autosport*, who decided that the following year the Cadets awards would be handed out at the *Autosport* Awards evening, and that I could receive some belated recognition by presenting the trophy to the 1992 winner. Mind you, one year later they forgot to invite me!

The *Autosport* Awards would become very important to me for another reason, but that still lay a long way in the future.

At the end of 1991 I moved up to an important category: Junior Britain. Their karts were bigger than Cadets, and where Cadets had a maximum of 5bhp, Junior Britain had 20. It was for kids between twelve and sixteen, so there were little tiddlers like me straight out of Cadets mixing it with older drivers who were starting to shave and have girlfriends. It was quite an odd mix, and we all had to comply to a minimum weight so that nobody gained an advantage through being small.

We stayed with Simon Wright and used Parilla engines. My first race was a week after the O Plate, at Clay Pigeon. I'd done no testing because Dad didn't want it to upset my driving style while I was still in Cadets, so it was all new to me. I just tested the day before the race, in the normal way. I know Dad was a bit shattered having to watch me move up into the bigger category, because it was a big step. I was entered in a good field too, among them Marc Hynes who was being run by karting legend Terry Fullerton. I qualified second for the final and went on to win it, even though it rained and I had never driven the kart before in the wet. It seemed to get a few people quite excited.

Then, the following week, there was the Junior O Plate at Clay. Dave Spence ran me, which was just as well because the karts were fast and tricky to set up. I was fourth or fifth fastest in testing on the Saturday, which seemed to upset some of the regulars. I got wiped out big time on the Sunday.

Dave was a fiery person. He once said to me at a race about another driver, 'Don't worry about it, John. That other kid is going nowhere. Just be calm. I know what you feel like, but it's not worth retaliating.' And his voice was just getting louder and louder, and with that he shot out of the awning. Let's put it politely: he went straight off and had words with this other driver! After that Steve Clayton, the Clerk of the Course at Clay, seriously considered disqualifying Jenson. The rule is that if the person who runs a driver does something that might reflect on the driver, he will be the one to suffer. Dave talked his way out of that one and carried on, but when we were reflecting on the meeting we all just thought, 'Wow, what are we up against?'

John Button

For 1992 I concentrated on Junior TKM, which had similar chassis to Junior Britain and restricted engines from TKM (Tal-Ko Motors) with about 16bhp. We used Wright chassis and Dad did the engines. We had three engines per race, and to help pay for my racing Dad always had one of them up for sale. Every meeting he sold one for a lot of money. This upset Neil Hann, the guy who was running me that season, but Dad would always come up with another quick motor, so we were OK. We also did a limited number of Junior Britain races, where Neil had lots of experience. Wherever we went we were quick, so we were all quite excited when we headed off for the first round of the British TKM Championship at Rowrah in April.

Rowrah is a mega circuit in an old quarry up in the Lake District, a real driver's track. During the race I found myself fighting for the lead with a Scottish kid by the name of McLaren. At one stage I went for the inside line on a corner. I just threw my kart down the inside sideways, hit his back wheel and sent him spinning, then I landed on him. It was my fault. I thought I'd have a go but it didn't quite work (a bit like Monza in 2001, really!).

I push-started the kart and carried on, but the guy's father had a real go at me. I've always cared what people thought of me, and his anger really got to me. It's horrible being shouted at, especially when you're only twelve years old. 'You can't drive,' he was screaming. 'You're crazy, a danger to everyone,' that sort of thing. And the thing was, I never crashed. Well, hardly ever. That was one of the only times that year. And I have to say it didn't teach me a lesson. I'd try exactly the same thing again because it was just an accident, a mistake. Everyone makes them from time to time. But that bollocking from McLaren senior upset me for the rest of the meeting and we had a terrible race.

Later on, when we got home, Dad and I talked through what had happened. The feelings and emotions of that day had faded, and I felt better. I decided that I wasn't going to be on the receiving end any more. I was going to be the one dishing it out, not aggressively or by being unpleasant to people, but by doing what I already knew how to do: driving well and winning. I wasn't going to let anything get to me again.

There was an interesting situation early in the season, when Jens learned an important lesson about racing. We were up at Rowrah in the Lake District, where there is a very good little circuit in an old quarry. Testing for the first round of the British Championship in TKM had gone ever so well for us and he was one of the quickest. But unfortunately in his first heat he had a coming-together with another kart, driven by a Scottish guy. It was a racing incident, but I have to say, being his father, that it wasn't Jens's fault. He lunged up the inside of the guy, who then turned in as they got to the apex.

When I got back to parc fermé the father was there giving Jens a real rollicking. The kid was upset, understandably, so I said my piece and put a stop to it. Nobody had ever spoken to him like that before.

The incident really rocked him for the rest of the event and he didn't get out of the B Final. He started fourth from last in the B Final, and that's where he finished. We were all left wondering what had happened to our big hopes for the championship. It was a very quiet drive home. And it's a very long way from Rowrah to Frome. We were all absolutely devastated.

To cap it all, we stopped to top up with fuel. It was really windy, the wind caught the car door and ripped it off its hinges. So we had fun and games at that one!

John Button

But I soon got over it. There were five races left in the British Championship, and we went out and dominated them to clinch the title. By the final race, I was already champion. It was highly satisfying after what had happened at Rowrah.

The next season, 1993, however, was a pretty bad one. I was doing Junior Britain full time now, but there were new, softer Bridgestone tyres and a different carburettor to slow things down a bit because the karts were so fast (despite that, on average, the karts were actually one and a half seconds quicker than the previous season). It was just a disastrous year when nothing went right for me. It was hard work, and the experience was a cold dose of reality for us: we were small privateers amid the big-buck teams run by the top guys with endless amounts of engines. The kart we were using was just a disaster. I also had to change my style slightly because I was doing things that didn't suit the engine. I was overheating it; I think we blew up twenty engines that year. Unbelievable. At one race I couldn't even do the final because I'd blown all three of my engines.

But over the winter of 1993/4 we managed to get a bit more money together, and then an invaluable chance came my way to iron out the problems with my driving style and widen my experience. Hopes quickly began to build for a good 1994.

THREE

TURNING PROFESSIONAL

In December 1993 we got a call from a guy called Sergen Popovic, a Serb based in Greece and apparently a successful businessman, who was looking to start up a new junior karting team in Italy. There was a ten-day test in Sicily, starting 2 January – would we like to go? It was a golden opportunity, because Dad simply couldn't finance overseas racing for me. We thought the guy was joking. But he was serious.

So we were going to Sicily. But we nearly didn't get there. From Frome we had to make our way to Heathrow airport. Well, it was winter, and a pretty cold one at that. Dad was driving an Audi Coupé back then. Just outside the village where we lived it was really icy, the roads like skating rinks with black ice. I can remember very clearly the lamp-post we were heading for, sideways. The surface was just sheet ice, nobody had been out gritting. Even a four-wheel-drive car couldn't cope, and Dad was no slouch at the wheel with all his rallycross experience (in fact, that was probably what saved us). To think it could all have ended there, at least as far as my racing was concerned. It was pretty scary, but every time we go past that lamp-post now we laugh and smile at each other. Maybe some day I'll get one of those blue plaques on it. 'John and Jenson Button just missed crashing into this lamp-post, 1 January 1994'.

We made the plane with about a second to spare, and the test in Sicily went very well. I was driving a kart for Team Rambo, run not, as you might imagine, by Sylvester Stallone but by a guy called Fabiano Belletti and his father Lamberto. Fabiano had been European Formula A champion, and this was the first time he and his father had run their own team. The guy in Greece, Sergio, was going to finance it all. If selected, we would compete in the Italian Championships, where it really does all happen, and the European and World Championships, plus a few other selected major events.

The setting was stunning, at the foot of Mount Etna, and Dad and I just gaped when we saw how much equipment they had. We were a bit worried about security out there, so they arranged for some locals to come along. They would arrive, open their car boots, and put rifles around their shoulders. Then they'd sit in the awnings, daring anyone to do anything wrong. You didn't need to be a genius to figure out what clan they belonged to! The locals also fed us well. Dad put on half a stone in just ten days.

It was a difficult test for me, because it was the first time I'd used super-soft tyres. Halfway through the first day I popped a rib out because of all the grip and the bumpiness of the circuit. The pain was horrible, and I just couldn't go out again until the last day, when it was raining.

Lamberto didn't speak any English, but he came to me, pointed to his eye, pointed to Jenson and to the circuit,

and made a sign with his hand which meant 'No problem', 'Very good', or whatever. Fabiano spotted something wrong with Jenson's driving. Everything was getting very hot, and what he was doing, which explained why we had lost so many engines the previous year in Junior Britain, was power braking. He'd picked that up in Cadets, where he would be braking for a corner but maintaining a certain amount of throttle. No problem in Cadets, where they rarely use the brakes, but with the extra power in Junior Britain the engine was driving against the brakes and not liking it. So we cured that there and then.

John Button

Despite all my problems we were offered a drive, together with two Greek drivers. The deal was that Team Rambo would pay for everything apart from hotels and air fares. That was really the start of my professional career. Racing in Britain was great, but this was a step up and I was getting everything paid for, which was really cool. Suddenly, as I turned the tender age of fourteen, I was a professional karter.

Naturally, Jenson missed a lot of school because of his racing, but I wasn't too worried because he's always been a bright lad and he didn't seem to be falling behind. When he was fourteen I went up to the middle school he was attending at the time to explain to the headmaster about all the time off he now needed in order to race in Europe. He already had two British Championships under his belt, but I don't know who was more amazed, me or them, when it transpired that none of his teachers or schoolmates had any idea what he'd been doing. He hadn't said a word.

John Button

Europe was an ultra-competitive arena. There were two categories in Italy, Cadet and Junior. The karts were identical, the split was just done on age. I was the youngest guy there, so I was in Cadets, with a 100cc Parilla-engined Birel chassis.

My first race was the Margutti Trophy at Parma in March, named after Andrea Margutti, a young Italian driver destined for the top who had died in a really crazy accident at the circuit six years earlier. This event was the warm-up for the season and everyone was there. We couldn't believe it when we drove to the circuit. There were Formula One style transporters everywhere; the professionalism was unbelievable. Rambo, now renamed Team Astra after the major sponsor, was a new team, well equipped, but the others were massive. And so were the names: Trulli, Fisichella, Manetti, Orsini, Gianniberti. The list went on and on. We suddenly realized where we were, and what we were up against. I'll never forget that time.

Those races in the Italian Championships were when I first started wearing my Union Jack helmet. Up until then I'd had a black helmet with yellow stripes, but to the Italians that summoned up images of the devil, so they said they would do me a new one.

The Cadet and Junior categories were run together for the Margutti Trophy, with around sixty-five entries. I was running sixth when I crashed in the pre-final so I qualified mid-field for the final, but I got wiped out in the first corner. When I finally got going again I went from last place to eleventh. With a lap to go I was up behind Kristian Kolby, a Danish driver against whom I would later race in Formula Three and whose sisters Ellen and Kirsten (who also raced) now work in public relations for McLaren and Williams respectively. I knew I couldn't win, but I wanted a top-ten finish so I tried a mega lunge that didn't quite come off. I went over the top of Kristian and took off his steering wheel, but I did finish tenth. Kristian wasn't very happy, but Team Astra was. They announced that they would now pay for my hotels and air fares too, which was a bonus.

I had a couple of shunts during that series, but I was competitive. And I wasn't alone: we introduced to Team Astra fellow Brits Tom Sisley, Westley Barber and Colin Brown, who would later go on to win the World Formula A Championship. I also competed in the winter series at Val Vibrata, but Dad didn't come out for that one. Initially Dad always travelled out with me on the Tuesday for races, and we'd return together the following Monday, but after a while, and once I'd got used to the routine, he only came out for the major races and I, at the age of fourteen, would travel to them on my own.

While he was in Britain a horrible tragedy occurred at Kimbolton in Cambridgeshire, one of the top British tracks, when Dave Spence's nine-year-old son Danny was killed in a freak Cadet accident on 11 December. The kart rolled and a rib punctured one of his lungs. The karting world was devastated. This tragedy was the trigger for every circuit to have paramedics on hand. It was something that was long overdue, even though karting is inherently a safe sport. Dad flew out to Italy soon after, and it must have been terrifying for him in the aftermath of Danny Spence's death to watch me racing. To make matters worse, he then witnessed another very serious accident in a Juniors race.

We were back in England, on the M4 driving back to Frome, when Dad finally told me about Danny. I just burst into tears. I couldn't believe it. The funeral was so sad, and the church was packed. People who couldn't get in were standing outside. At the Spences' house afterwards Dave was a rock. I was still very upset, but he took me into another room and spoke to me for fifteen minutes, helping me to get my head around the tragedy. It was the first time in my life I'd ever encountered anything so harrowing.

That year I learned a lot of valuable lessons, on and off the track. The last of them had come in the pre-final of the CIK 5 Continents Cup for Juniors, the 'junior world championship', at Ugento in southern Italy in July. I had worked up to third place, but then I messed up. I pushed a bit too hard in one corner and got up onto two wheels; there was so much rubber on the circuit that I just went off. That was down to inexperience, and it made me think even harder about how much there was still to learn.

In Cadets in Italy a lot of people didn't realize just how quick Jenson was. He was with a new team, and just stupid little problems kept arising. You couldn't go and tell anyone because they sounded like excuses. Jenson was in Cadets and Giorgio Pantano was in Juniors. Giorgio had been racing in Italy for quite some time and was the Great White Hope. But Jenson was matching his times, even though it was really early days and he was in Cadets. So that was our measure. But there were accidents, punctures, engine seizures, carburettors going down, all that sort of stuff. But we knew it was there, and the right people noticed it.

John Button

Dad and I were paying our dues. And believe me, whoever you are in motor racing, you have to go through that. The unwritten law is that you can never win every race. It just doesn't happen. Of course you have to go into every race believing that you can win, but when you don't there's no point getting yourself all twisted up because you weren't successful this time. You just have to accept that law and move on. Look ahead to the next one, and get the job done there. Even if you get into one of those spells when it seems you just can't do anything right. All the angst, all the disappointment, all the times when you come away with your chin on the floor – and we've been there, many times, just like all the other guys I've raced against – those are the down payments you make on a career in the sport.

I don't believe that anybody wins any race purely through luck. It might play its part, but it is only a part, even if the guy in front throws his chain on the last corner and you nip past for the win. When you get out onto a track to compete with everyone else and get yourself into a position where you can win, then you have achieved something through your own efforts and those of the team you race with. It doesn't matter whether it's a works outfit or the team you and your dad have created so that you can go racing. You have stood up to be counted. You've done something. I think that is terribly important. Instead of watching from the sidelines you have taken a step towards realizing your dream. It's crucial. Nobody achieves anything by sitting on their bum carping from the sidelines. You have to stand up to be counted in the first place. You have to be prepared to expose yourself to criticism and disappointment. Like I said, they are down payments, and you should consider them as such. Because, believe me, the feelings you get when you start winning are worth every bit of disappointment, every single car journey home after a bad meeting when neither you nor your dad can think of anything cheerful to say.

I suppose I have become something of a role model to young karters, who have seen through me that it really is possible to progress through the ranks and get to Formula One. It's the same with guys such as my former team-mate at Benetton Giancarlo Fisichella, or my new partner Jarno Trulli, Jos Verstappen or Kimi Raikkonen. The majority of my Formula One peers, in fact. Nearly all of them came out of karting, starting when they were kids and working away at it. Of course, they all have a very high level of skill

– without it they wouldn't have been given the breaks – but all of them are shining examples of what's possible if you are dedicated enough to keep pushing yourself forwards. And fortunate enough to get the right breaks at the right time, of course. Another thing you learn very quickly as a young kart racer is that you will never get anywhere without help. You just cannot climb the mountain without assistance. It's an essential element in the success equation, and it comes in many forms.

Despite our problems with the kart I came fourth in the 1994 RAC British Junior Championship, even though I decided part of the way through the season that I'd done enough racing in Britain, having won my first JICA (Junior Inter-Continental Formula A) race in Europe and two races in the Italian JICA winter series. In 1995 I was going to move up to Juniors, but the organizers changed the age splits so I had to move up even further. I couldn't progress to Formula A because fellow Brit Doug Bell was Team Astra's Formula A driver, so I went into Senior ICA, one step below Formula A.

We competed in the Italian Championships in ICA with a Birel powered by Rotax engines prepared by Paul Lemmens, and I scored almost twice as many points as the guy who finished runner-up. That was pretty satisfying, but things were difficult on another front. The Italian teams run drivers from all over the world, but they like them to race on Italian licences so that when they win, they win for Italy. I wasn't prepared to do that. I'm British, and I'm proud of it. This attitude brought its own problems, particularly on one occasion when I was sitting on the front row of the grid for a final and my kart was taken to parc fermé where the organizers drained it of its fuel and substituted some of their own. I just made the grid in time, then had trouble getting the fuel up on the warm-up lap. And I got disqualified at Parma in one of my last Senior ICA races. The chain had broken during one heat and had slightly damaged part of the plastic cover that protects the electrics. We were informed that the engine no longer matched the original drawings. Even the Italian engine tuners said that was too much! Eventually, though, the Italians accepted my right to be a British driver racing abroad and left me alone. They even started calling me 'the young lion', which was quite flattering. I was now Buttoni, a bit like the pasta-makers!

At this time Jenson was at Frome College, and they didn't even know he was kart racing. He never talked about it there either. When they found out I was called in and we discussed how his education should go, how they could help. They were really, really good. They said if he was in athletics, they would be expected to help, and they looked on karting the same way.

John Button

Towards the end of 1995 I took part in the European Championships at St Amond, a stunning part of the south of France. Most teams had huge problems with tyre wear, so much so that the CRG team pulled out after a lap of the pre-final to save their rubber. I was on pole for that race, a couple of tenths quicker than anyone else, but everyone in the team was depressed because they knew my tyres wouldn't make it through. Sure enough, they didn't.

Then there was the Formula A World Championship meeting at Valence in France in September. I hadn't qualified for it, but Paul Lemmens had spent a long time persuading Ernst Buser, the president of world karting, that I should be allowed to race. At the eleventh hour he agreed. I was to drive a works Tecno chassis with one of Paul's tuned Rotax engines and Bridgestone tyres, running for Paul's GKS team. It was during this time that I first met Jos

Verstappen. Sophie Kumpen, who is now Jos's wife, was also racing for Paul in Super A. She was a quick driver. (With that pedigree their son Max, who is four, should be a mega driver in years to come!)

In those days Bridgestone made standard and special tyres. The top guys qualified for the special rubber, but we didn't have it because we hadn't raced in Europe all year. Obviously that was going to put us at a disadvantage, because the special tyres were stickier and therefore generated greater grip, but we were told that if we were among the twenty best heat runners then Bridgestone would give us the special tyres for the pre-final and the final. Well, that was a challenge, and I've always liked challenges. I managed to record the eighteenth best time, so we were given the special tyres. I went out on them and immediately began to lap faster than the Super A guys had done. Unfortunately I blew my best engine in the morning warm-up session, but Paul worked some magic and I was ready to roll.

Those special tyres had to last for the pre-final and the final, however. In the pre-final I got involved in an incident on the first lap and dropped back to about twenty-second place, but I managed to come back and win the race. Really, I should have been satisfied with a top-four placing and saved the tyres for the final, but the thrill of winning can be intoxicating and I pushed too hard, too eager to catch the three leaders. That performance really set the paddock buzzing, because it was so unexpected. The track is like an amphitheatre and there were lots of British fans there, so it was fantastic.

I started from pole for the final and I led for twenty-three out of the twenty-four laps, but they were the wrong twenty-three. By the last five my tyres had gone off. The Brazilian driver Gustav Fraguas got past me on the final lap, so I finished vice-champion to him. But no regrets. It was a fantastic race, and it was a great experience to race with Paul, his wife Lisette and their son Koen, and my super-enthusiastic mechanic Alex. It was a really happy little team.

In 1996 I went into Formula A full time in Europe with Paul Lemmens, and I was installed as one of the favourites. I didn't mind that. Some guys hate that kind of pressure of expectation, but it's never bothered me. I like the attention. It's good for the ego, and it's quite a good psychological edge to have over the opposition. But the season turned into another nightmare.

The tyre regulations had changed again, and the organizers had introduced across-the-board control tyres. Bridgestone supplied the sort of hard-compound tyre any manufacturer would introduce in such circumstances, because there is rarely any point in supplying anything else when you don't have any opposition. When there is no incentive to develop a competitive edge, you opt for durability and longevity. You play it safe. Unfortunately, the Tecno chassis we had that year didn't like hard tyres, and we really suffered. It was very tough.

To make matters worse, part of the way through the year the sponsor's payments stopped. Paul stepped in to save us and told Dad and me not to worry. Without his words of support and his offer to cover all my expenses, my career would have stalled there and then. It was a fantastic gesture, one I really appreciated. It was a major boost for me that year, as was the contribution of Alex, my mechanic. He was a very emotional man who dedicated himself 100 per cent to making my kart go faster. If anything went wrong with it he had tears in his eyes and took it as a personal failure. You can't put a price on working with such people.

I finished fifth in the championship, but it really was a struggle. The kart was an animal on those hard tyres, very difficult to drive – for the most part, anyway. Two races from the end of the campaign one of the team mechanics set about the kart with a hacksaw and cut through one of the frame tubes, then taped it over. Well, whatever he did transformed the kart and the final two races were fun, even if the kart did like to get up on two wheels a bit too much. But overall, 1996 was a disappointing season, despite a fifth place in the European Formula A Championship, a third in the American Championship at Charlotte in Georgia (which was a gas!), and another third in the World Cup at Suzuka in Japan, a race during which I had the biggest shunt of my career to date.

I was running third in one heat, chasing James Courtney (a Jaguar F3 driver in 2001) and thinking about where I was going to pass him. We were nearing the end of the long straight, so I took a quick peek over my shoulder to see where the next guy was just before having a lunge at James. At the very moment I was looking behind me, James's engine seized. He, of course, slowed dramatically, I ran straight into him, my kart flipped and came to rest on the track facing the wrong way. That was no fun at all, having to sit there and watch thirty karts screaming towards me. Most of them just nicked by either side, but right at the back there were two guys. One was a Scandinavian who hit my left front wheel, flipped and broke an arm as he crashed onto the grass. The other was a Japanese guy who had his head right down, in order to minimize his aerodynamic profile down the straight. He looked up just in the last moment before he hit my kart head-on. His kart rode right up and over mine, and as it did so its underside punctured my fuel tank and smacked me hard on the helmet, slamming my head right back over the seat. It's the classic way to break your neck, since the seat only comes up to below your shoulders. I was carted off, only partly conscious, to the medical unit, but I was lucky.

I'd hurt one of my legs in the shunt, but the spare kart was ready for the next heat and the team lifted me into it. I was second in that race, trying really hard not to let the pain get to me, but I only qualified to start from the back of the grid for the final because an engine sprocket had worked loose in the pre-final. I fought up to third place and finished there, but this position was disputed because I'd overtaken two guys at the back before we'd reached the flag that started the race. Everyone does that in karting and normally nobody worries about it. Ernst Buser told me he'd seen the video and pronounced that no action would be taken, so I was allowed to keep my position. He wanted to award me the Ayrton Senna Memorial Cup, but felt that because of the minor infringement he couldn't do that. In some ways I'd rather have had the cup than third place, but I made amends for that a year later.

Over the winter we received a number of offers to join bigger teams for 1997, which I was hoping would be my last season in karts. I would be graduating full time to Formula Super A, the Formula One of karting, but you can't just turn up and race in it. Like Formula One, you have to qualify for it, and I had done that on the strength of my 1996 performances. The decision we had to take was who to run with. Tecno was a small manufacturer; our other options were the dominant CRG and TonyKart teams. It was left to me to make the decision, on the basis that I was the one who had to drive whatever kart we chose. CRG and TonyKart were tempting, of course, but I had a great relationship with Paul Lemmens and GKS and I believed that Tecno could do the job, so I decided to stay with them. I'd spent a lot of time with Paul and his family out in Genk, just an hour's drive east of Brussels, where Paul runs a kart track, and I just liked working with him. Maybe they couldn't offer as much as CRG or TonyKart, who were the major-league players, the Williams and Ferrari of the Formula A game, but it worked out, and that was enormously satisfying. I place a high premium on loyalty, and I was really happy that the decision to follow my heart paid off. I was really pleased that we could enjoy success with Tecno against the giants. Paul did us a very good deal and really looked out for my interests.

I passed my driving test in 1997 too, which was liberating, as any seventeen-year-old will tell you. I first drove my dad's car, on an airfield, sitting on his lap, when I was eight. I took my first test after just five lessons – and failed! The examiner said I went through a gap that just wasn't there. I think maybe I scared him, because it seemed OK to me. There were two cars parked on my side of the road and another car coming the other way. There were definitely a few inches to spare, but the other car felt it had to go up the kerb to avoid me ... I passed second time around, though, and got myself a Vauxhall Cavalier to bomb around in when I was in England. It had a two-litre fuel-injected engine, seventeen-inch wheels, stiff suspension and a nice loud stereo. Proper boy-racer style. Not quite what I have to play with now, but I really loved that car. It was cool.

Jenson did have a tendency to go a bit fast. They like you to leave about ten feet between you and the car in front. Jenson left three inches.

Roger Brunt, driving instructor

I started the 1997 season off by winning the Winter Cup, a warm-up for the main European Championship, and then went on to become the first British driver, and the youngest ever, to win the European Formula Super A Championship. It was run over four circuits, with two races per meeting at each. I was up against all the big names who had been there a long time, plus Giorgio Pantano, the new Italian kid on the block. It was incredibly competitive. One small mistake, one lunge that didn't come off, and you'd lose ten places just like that. Fantastic racing.

At Garda in northern Italy for my first race I was on the front row, but I had a really hard time in the race and came away without any points. We were all a bit down, just like that time at Rowrah in TKM, but we all discussed it and I learned a valuable lesson: I had to toughen up on the track, and a change in tactics had to help me do that.

The second round was held at Salbris in France, a big, fast circuit. I won the first final by a big margin, and in the second Pantano was charging and came up behind me halfway through. I knew he wasn't going to take any prisoners so I let him through and chased him, just watching what was happening. That was part of the lesson I'd learned from Garda. I could see his tyres were starting to go, and two laps from home I did a massive lunge on him, made sure he stayed out in the dirt, and won. That gave me maximum points, which was very satisfying.

We couldn't get the kart working well for the third round at Valence in September, but at one stage I was running third in the middle of a big fight. I couldn't get the kart out of the corners fast enough so I was getting passed on the straight, but I'd outbrake them into the corners. With a lap to go Palmieri was getting upset behind me, then he tried an impossible move and ended up T-boning me and driving over my feet, so that was another non-score.

The final round was at Genk, Paul's home circuit. I'd done a lot of testing there so I knew the place intimately. There were five or six of us fighting for the title, but I was the only non-Italian. A friend of Paul's had just opened up a refurbished chateau, so we stayed there for the duration. It was unbelievable; the rooms were enormous. You could have played tennis in those bedrooms!

The heats went well. I paced myself, knowing that I didn't need to win everything. The finals were what mattered. I was leading the first final, in the damp, from Pantano, when he went for a big lunge and edged me out onto the dirt. It was payback for Salbris. So it all came down to the last final. Giorgio only had an outside chance of taking the title; all I had to do was finish fourth to become champion. I started on the front row, still on a wet track, but before I got into the kart I went up to Dad and said, 'If I get round that first corner, I'm going to be champion. But I don't think they're going to let me.' I was nervous because this race was the culmination of everything we'd worked for together over the past ten years. Everything rested on it. When I got back to the grid all my Italian rivals were there, pointing at me, at the circuit, trying to outpsych me. Dad went down to the first corner so that if I was wiped out he could see who had done it.

We did the warm-up lap, all of us giving it loads of throttle then braking hard to warm the tyres. The guy on pole, Davide Fore, was also up for the title. At one point he accelerated then braked quickly, and I hit him in the back. He obviously thought that was a wind-up, so he let me through and gave me a whack. Things were pretty tense by the time we got to the start.

I was second going into the first corner on a very slippery wet track, but I went in a little bit too quick because I was trying to open up a gap to the guys behind. I clipped the kerb and ended up in the gravel trap on the outside. I kept my foot flat on the throttle and on its treaded wet tyres the kart gradually dragged itself out. I set off after everyone. Halfway round I came upon another coming together, so I avoided the guys involved by going into the gravel again. I was in about twentieth place at this stage, and angry as hell with myself. I just got my head down, and began to carve my way through the field.

Eventually I got back up to fourth, which was all I needed to secure the title, but I didn't want to rely on other people's mathematics. Fore and his TonyKart team-mate had disappeared, so I went after Orsini in third place and passed him. But then the two TonyKart guys began slowing up. Winning wasn't enough for Fore if I finished fourth, so his team-mate was riding shotgun for him, waiting for me. Dad was frantically waving at me to slow down as I was beginning to catch them, so every time they slowed down I just went slower to foil their game. Behind me, meanwhile, Orsini was closing in, so I still couldn't relax. When we crossed the line we were all bumper to bumper. If there'd been another lap, who knows what might have happened?

I'd done enough to clinch the title, and there was a massive celebration afterwards. I'd done something no British driver had ever done, and I was the youngest Super A champion there had ever been. There was only one thing left to do. We had shaken hands on a deal earlier in the year that if I won the European title I had to shave my head. So out came the scissors and razor!

Some good friends of ours, Jim Rainbird, his partner Julie and John Beacham, all of them big supporters through my karting career, were there, as well as Dad and Pippa. There were a lot of tears. I picked up four massive cups, one for each final, one for driver of the day and one for European champion, and we drove home from Genk in a BMW 7-series with all this silverware in the back window. We had a mega race for the ferry, and celebrated all the way home. It was just a fantastic day.

That year I could also have won the Super A World Championship, the Blue Riband of karting. In those days it was a one-off event, held that year at Salbris in France. I knew the track well from the European rounds there, so I was optimistic. Things were fine in the heats, and come the final I soon found myself sitting behind Alessandro Manetti in second place, just biding my time and feeling pretty comfortable. He was going for it, but I was just sitting there on his bumper. I wasn't even crouching down on the straight to minimize drag, just sitting upright, choking the engine, pulling away with Manetti from the rest of the field. There was absolutely no point at that stage in starting a fight with him. I was just playing a waiting game, waiting for the right moment to make my move in the last couple of laps. Until then I was going to be content to work with him to make sure we dropped everyone else.

And then, after only three laps, the engine seized. It happened on a fast part of the circuit, right in front of Dad. I went off the track, bounced across the grass and into the barriers, ending up about a metre from where he was standing.

I'd gone to that event feeling really confident. I knew I could become world champion. I just knew it inside. I'd gone through a lot of disappointments in my karting career, but I just had this inner feeling that I could be world champion. And then that happened. I was so bitterly disappointed. My head dropped that time, because I knew it was going to be my last year in karting. As far as I was concerned, the championship had been there for the taking.

I was also out of luck again in Japan. In the semi-final of the World Cup I had to start from eighteenth spot on the grid after the front sprocket had shattered in one of the heats and prevented me from qualifying better, but I managed to work my way up to second. I was contesting the lead in the final when the chain broke. But at least this time my efforts won me the Ayrton Senna Memorial Cup, which made up for the disappointment of not being allowed to accept it the previous year.

Some people will tell you that a good loser is a permanent loser, but I disagree. Like I said, you can't win every race even if you go into them all with the intention of winning. I admit, though, that I'm a bad loser. I just don't like losing. But I've never been one for the tearful tantrums that you see so often in karting. I've never been one of those drivers who throw their gloves on the ground in frustration. That's totally not me. I just don't think that sort of thing is necessary. Dad never brought me up that way; it's bred in me not to behave like that. You win some, you lose some. And those you lose you just use to strengthen your resolve even more to win in the future. I hate losing, but when I do I try to do it with grace. You put a false smile on and you use the knockback as a means of motivating yourself even more. If you throw a tantrum other drivers see it, and it plays into their hands.

That afternoon in Salbris at the Super A World Championship final, I stood there with Dad by the side of the track after I'd come to a halt, and though I felt like crying, I didn't. Instead, I looked him straight in the eye and just said, 'Dad, wait until the next bloody race.'

I know that Ayrton Senna was always frustrated by the fact that he never managed to win the karting World Championship. But though I was really disappointed at the time, I have never let it eat away at me the way it ate away at him. When I look back now, it doesn't bother me that I didn't win it. I've read comments by Jarno Trulli and others who rate their best victories in the European Championship because it's contested over eight races, whereas the World Championship was then just a one-off. And I agree with them. I think the European Championship was in its own way a better measure.

By the time I was ready to move into cars I think it's fair to say that there was growing interest in what I was doing. The karting magazines had always been very good to me, but now I was getting some press in the specialist motor racing magazines as well. A friend of ours, Steve Fellows, who owned a motorsport promotions company called Proaction and had taken an interest in me over the years, trying to help in finding sponsorship for us, called and said, 'Now it's going to happen. Now the sponsors are going to come out.' (As it turned out, offers weren't exactly thick on the ground.) But to be honest, when I was in karting I tried not to think about the future too much. I just wanted to concentrate on what I could achieve.

That's not to say I didn't know what I wanted out of life. By the time I was eight years old I had decided that I wanted to be a Formula One driver. That was when the goal began to define itself in my mind and become the focus of my existence. It took priority over everything else. I started watching my weight, even gave up chocolate, and worried that I was growing too much. In the end I topped out at six feet, and I weigh 74kg, so I'm OK.

One of the things I remember reading in the national papers when I got into Formula One was that I hogged an entire assembly on one occasion when we had to talk about sports we were into. I'm supposed to have held sway for ages, telling everyone that I was going to become a Formula One driver. Well, it may have been what I was aiming for at the time, but that's not the way I remember it. What I recall was that when I was twelve years old I was wheeled into the old assembly hall in my brm-brm kart, with my helmet and overalls on. They opened the curtains, I came out, and they closed them again. I just sat there. I didn't say a thing. I was far too embarrassed. I had the chance to, but there was no way I would have done that. As for me hogging assembly and telling everyone I was going to be world champion, no way. I never used to say anything about my racing. You do that when you're a kid. You avoid anything that makes you feel different.

I knew Formula One was where I wanted to be, I just didn't know when it would happen. It wasn't just some nebulous thought hanging around in my head. That's what I wanted my career to be, 100 per cent. It was either school or racing then. I did parts of the courses, and the schools I went to were very understanding and tolerant about my racing, but I didn't do much because I was away racing so much. I never did any exams, so it's good that things have worked out for me. Now I've got everything but Formula One race wins. I don't have to worry about money or anything. I'm racing against the best drivers in the world. I'm just not beating them all yet.

So I owe a great deal to karting. It laid the groundwork for my subsequent career in cars, and it taught me so much: how to handle a racing machine; how to drive quickly yet safely; how a fast vehicle feels at speed when the front or back end is right on, or over; the limits to tyre adhesion; how to race in company; how to conduct myself on and off the track; how to be self-confident and self-sufficient. Without karting I could never have been successful in cars.

Karting is the perfect arena in which to hone driving skills, especially as you can start racing as early as eight years old. I know a lot of guys who started driving karts long before that, with big wooden blocks on the pedals. It's like skiing and other such sports: the earlier you start doing them the better you become in the long term. Kids pick up things much faster than adolescents or adults do. People marvel at how mature young racing drivers are these days, especially when they jump into Formula One just after their nineteenth or twentieth birthday. But it's not such a surprise when they go well if you consider that many of them have been racing for eight or nine years by the time they find their way into racing cars. There's nothing like racing other guys wheel-to-wheel at 60mph, an inch off the ground and only inches apart, to make you grow up in a hurry.

FOUR

ON THE NURSERY SLOPES

In any form of racing, you won't get anywhere without the right people behind you. When you come out of karting it can be very difficult to choose the route to take in cars, because it's usually an alien environment. After eight years you tend to know everyone in karting; suddenly you are confronted with a whole new bunch of people. Who can you trust? Who will do the best job for you? Who will try to rip you off? Who should you avoid like the plague? I've always been very fortunate to have Dad there to bounce ideas off, and as car racing beckoned two other key figures came into the picture: David Robertson and Harald Huysman, who became my managers. Keith Sutton, one of the sport's top photographers, also played a pivotal role, helping me with publicity, just the way he had two decades earlier with Ayrton Senna.

Dad and I had tried to get a budget together to enable us to make the move from karts to cars, and one guy, Paul Lambert, came along and offered to finance me through his motorsport company to do a year in Formula Ford. We spoke to Van Diemen, a front-running manufacturer for many seasons, and although they didn't have any seats left in their works team they offered to set up a satellite effort. We didn't like the sound of that, so we contacted a team called Haywood Racing. They hadn't yet won a championship, but they used the French Mygale chassis, which was going very well. One of their big assets was a guy called Malcolm Pullen, whom everyone called Puddy. What he didn't know about Formula Ford wasn't worth knowing; his association with the sport went right back to Van Diemen's halcyon years with Ayrton Senna. So we did some tests with them, and I was soon on the pace. I had a good run with my old karting partner Dan Wheldon during a test at Donington in December 1997, when he closed in on me and I then began to pull away again. That was encouraging, but then we hit a crisis: Jim Warren, who owns Haywood Racing, called to say that he hadn't received any money from Paul. He said they could carry on testing me, but I wouldn't be doing any racing until some money came through.

We had to be with a top team to avoid a career stall, so we were in some trouble. It began to look as if I would have to stay in karts for another year. I really didn't want to do that because it was time to move up. We did have a tentative offer from an agent of Flavio Briatore at Benetton, but back then it all seemed a bit premature and we politely declined.

Things have a habit of happening by themselves. We were worrying about the future, but unknown to us Harald Huysman was talking with Paul Lemmens. Harald wanted to build his own track out in Norway, had contacted Paul for advice, and Paul had gone to Norway to help him to design the circuit. On the way back to the airport Harald asked Paul who were the best three kart drivers he'd ever seen; Paul replied, 'Not three, two. Ayrton Senna and Jenson Button.' Harald had heard of Ayrton Senna, of course, but he hadn't a clue who I was. Paul explained what I had done in karting. Harald then told Paul that he had a friend in England, David Robertson, who was looking for a young driver to take through to Formula One. We didn't know who David was, but apparently he had the finances in place.

It all goes back to a conversation I had with Harald Huysman in America, when my son Steve was racing in Indy Lights there. Harald was in the same team, with Steve Horne at Tasman Motorsports. Steve was making a comeback and using Indy Lights as a stepping stone to CART. I said to Harald that there was so much talent out there that never really gets a chance, and I wouldn't mind helping somebody through. Guys really struggled without budgets. They either hit on something lucky or they didn't, so there was a lot of good talent going to waste. In England there is no real school for these guys to progress through.

In the end we decided to look at the karting world. I spoke to someone in England and Harald spoke to a guy from Belgium. I spoke to Terry Fullerton, who was the only karter Ayrton Senna really feared. Harald spoke to Paul Lemmens. Things didn't happen immediately, but some time later Harald was setting up a kart track in Norway and called on Paul for his expertise. Things went from there.

David Robertson, former joint manager

Paul rang us and told us to expect a phone call. It came in the middle of February. David was a bit secretive about who he was, but asked if we could be at Pembrey in Dyfed, Wales, in two days' time for a test in a Formula Three car. Before he committed himself, David wanted to see me drive a car, because not all karters can make the transition. At this stage he was talking of my jumping straight into Formula Three because experience of slicks and wings would be of greater benefit in the long term. He sent his son Steve, who had raced and won in Formula Three in the 1980s, to monitor my progress.

I confess that while we were driving to Wales I told Dad I thought it was all a wind-up, and that even if it wasn't it would result in a drive with a crappy Formula Three team. I was wrong. The outfit was Carlin Motorsport, one of the top teams, the car one of their Dallara Mugen-Hondas. It was all kept very secret because of the delicate situation with Paul Lambert. We hadn't actually signed an agreement with him, but one was on the table.

I had some private worries as well about moving up to Formula Three straight away. Compared to Formula Fords, Formula Three cars are light years ahead. They use 220bhp two-litre production-derived engines to keep costs down, but otherwise they are to all intents and purposes miniature Formula One cars, with carbon-fibre composite monocoque chassis, just like their bigger brothers, sophisticated suspension and electronics and wide slick tyres. They operate on similar aerodynamic principles too. It was that last point that worried me initially, before I even sat in one, because I simply didn't have any experience at all of vehicles with wings. Karts don't have any aerodynamics worth talking about. I was a bit nervous because you hear so many stories. Some people will tell you that it's just like a normal car but the wings help you a bit in corners. It's really strange: you just don't know how much to push yourself because of the aerodynamics. In a Formula Ford you push yourself to the limit of the tyres and the actual chassis; in Formula Three you push it past that because the aerodynamics help you. You have to find the limit of the aerodynamics. It's very tough. You can actually push a lot harder than you think, but gauging it takes a bit of time, so that's what I was worried about.

However, once I was in the car I felt completely at home. I actually got used to it on the first lap. It was just faster than anything I'd driven up to that point, that's all. In the cockpit you don't really notice the extra speed and power because the car is capable of handling it. I was able to get right on the pace almost immediately.

I'd heard all the hype about him before we gave him a test, and I was prepared to be sceptical. But I have to say I was highly impressed. He adapted so easily, it was hard to believe that he had so little experience in cars. You might have expected him to be unused to downshifting gears, but he wasn't flustered at all. At Pembrey you can hear the engine note all round the circuit, and his downshifts were superb. He did a fantastic job, and was only two tenths off Warren Hughes's best lap. He drove within himself, was very sensible and stayed calm. He had it all under control. He was as good as anyone I've seen on their first Formula Three run. He was calm and professional, and clearly had a big future ahead of him.

Trevor Carlin, owner, Carlin Motorsport

My son Steve won races in his time in Formula Three, and after the test he said to me, 'The kid is good. He's got good composure, he's relaxed, very smooth. He doesn't look like he's doing the times he's doing.'

David Robertson

Shortly after the Pembrey test David invited Dad and me to London to discuss a contract. We took one away, had it checked over, and decided to go for it. It meant signing away quite a big piece of my future, but it was a golden opportunity to get into car racing, so we signed. David wanted me to go straight into Formula Three, but I said no to that. Then he said it had to be Van Diemen if we went to Formula Ford, but I pushed hard for Haywood Racing and managed to persuade David that it was the right way to go. We finally agreed a deal quite late in the day, on 8 April just before the season kicked off.

So right from the start of my car career I had the right people around me. Jim Warren at Haywood Racing knows a great deal about the sport, about how to get the best out of the cars and his drivers. He was the perfect guide in my first season, though obviously I had ideas of my own that I also wanted to try. Jim coped with that too!

The logical category in which to race was the British Formula Ford Championship. Formula Ford caters for 1800cc single-seaters powered by Ford's four-cylinder Zetec engine from its range of road cars. That might not seem such a big deal, but when you install a 160bhp engine in an open-wheeled, torpedo-shaped, tubular-steel spaceframe chassis cloaked in glass-fibre bodywork, you have a lightweight missile that holds your attention.

It's funny, but a lot of karters hate Formula Fords when they first try them. A kart is usually a stiff little piece of kit, whereas the car is a lot heavier. It doesn't have the same directness and positivity that karts have. The steering is less precise. The car has suspension and gears. It rolls a lot more in corners, which some initially find off-putting. You've gone from your comfortable position close to the top of the karting world, and suddenly you're confronted with this peculiar animal that doesn't always behave the way you expect or want it to. It can be something of a culture shock, even though it's still just another vehicle with an engine, a steering wheel, four wheels and four tyre contact patches to help it go round corners. The thing you really shouldn't ever do is compare a Formula Ford to a kart. I used to do it myself at first, but really, they're so completely different that there's no point. You just have to adapt.

Changing horses was OK for me. I experienced no real problems once I'd got used to that difference in feel. In fact, I found the cars much simpler to set up than the karts. On the latter there's a lot more you can fiddle around with, such as varying the width of the track, loosening or tightening the sidepods and bumpers to change the way the chassis handles, playing around with the carburation. On the Ford you tend to leave the engine alone and focus on adjusting the suspension for maximum cornering grip, or altering the gear ratios.

A lot of racing drivers say that Formula Ford is very boring to drive compared to a kart, but I like any sort of fast machine. Of course, karting is always very exciting because you're exposed on top of this piece of welded-up tube and are sitting so low to the ground. But whatever I drive I always want to go faster with every lap, so it really doesn't matter what it is as far as I'm concerned.

It's not easy to adjust to Formula Ford from karting, with the Zetec engines and slicks, but Jenson did a great job. He never got ragged or ruffled. He stayed focused and he was clear-minded. He was quick straight out of the box at Thruxton, though he'd never been there or driven a Formula Ford before. That was amazing, possibly even better than David Coulthard was there in similar circumstances. But the big difference is that where others struggle when things go bad, he stayed calm and didn't overdrive. What impressed me most was that no matter what the circumstance, he always seemed to be capable of going up another gear.

Jim Warren, manager, Haywood Racing

I adjusted quickly to my new role. My first race was that two-day meet at Thruxton, the old airfield circuit in Hampshire, on 12 and 13 April 1998, and amazingly it snowed just before the start. It's a very quick track, especially out the back, but things went well for me and afterwards I thought I'd do OK as far as speed was concerned. But I hadn't raced against many of the drivers, and Formula Ford at this level is always intensely competitive because it attracts the best drivers from all over the world. It's recognized as the breeding ground for new talent. It's the car-racing category that gave the world drivers such as Emerson Fittipaldi and Ayrton Senna. I wasn't sure exactly how good the other teams and drivers would be, but I was sure I had a very good chance of being up the front. A lot of people told me there was no chance of winning in my first year of Formula Ford, but I was absolutely determined to prove them wrong. I couldn't see why that would be the case.

I finished third behind my team-mate Derek Hayes in that first race. He blocked me a lot, which made me pretty angry, but I soon realized that I was into a new realm of motor racing that wasn't like karting. Blocking was the norm.

Jenson is very talented. It's very difficult to compare people, because so much depends on the competition, and you can only relate people to their immediate competition. But he took to single-seaters very quickly. He and Derek Hayes were really pushing each other along as team-mates, and both were finding time in themselves if the other went quicker.

Malcolm 'Puddy' Pullen, Haywood engineer

It was soon clear that other people expected me to be a threat. Some said I was the favourite. I wasn't sure that I was, because that's not the way I tend to think. I thought people saw Daniel Wheldon as the top driver. He was quick. Either way, it didn't bother me. But there's always a flipside to things like that. Early on at Silverstone, the venue for my second race, I found all sorts of guys slowing down so that I would overtake them in practice; then they'd tag along behind me and see where I was gaining time on them. That's all right up to a point, but it soon gets a bit annoying, especially when they do it purposely so that on your flying lap they slow you down, and then on their flying lap they get behind you so they can slipstream you and go quicker. You're lucky if you can get that sort of tow, because most people will slow down or go into the pits and straight out the exit again, so all they really did was slow us all up and jeopardize our chances of qualifying well.

I was having such big problems with all that, with having my chances of going quicker messed up so often by this sort of behaviour, that I came into the pits and told the team it was ridiculous to stay out there. There was no point carrying on until the track was clearer. I didn't think my decision was any big deal; it was just logic that came from karting. You learn so much there. It's a world like Formula One, from the engineering aspects to racecraft. I just knew I would go quicker when the traffic died down.

That time at Silverstone, Jenson had done only ten laps in practice, then he came in and waited almost until the end of the session. He and his team-mate Derek Hayes were within three thousandths of a second of one another and Jenson came in to ask how far away he was. He let the tyres cool a little and the traffic quieten down, then calmly said, 'I'd best go out and do something about it.' Within two laps he had taken pole, and he went on to

win his first Formula Ford victory that day. I thought he showed remarkable judgement and calmness, biding his time that way. It was obvious that besides being quick he was also very smart and confident in himself.

Jim Warren

After my victory at Silverstone, the championship momentum swung my way until I was docked a victory at Brands for overtaking Wheldon going into Druids. There was a yellow flag directly in front of Dan, but obscured from my view as I went for the inside. It was one of those things, but nobody was going to come to my support in the circumstances. I got kicked out of the whole meeting for that, though, which I thought was rather draconian.

As I said, I didn't ever regard myself as the favourite in Formula Ford because I was the new boy and lacked experience. And things were pretty relaxed in that direction – until I started winning races. The first couple of races people said I only won because other drivers crashed. Yeah, true, but they crashed and I didn't. Then I started winning races from the front, and people got a bit excited about it.

I don't think any of the other drivers liked the publicity I was starting to get. The magazines were giving me a lot of coverage, and the teams weren't happy, especially the drivers who had been there a year or two. They didn't fully know what to expect of me, and they didn't like all the attention going my way. But it happens; people other than me have been on the receiving end of a lot of publicity in Formula Ford. You just have to roll with it.

I suppose I was used to it, because in karting I'd been the first Briton to win the European Championship in Super A. That was a big thing, and the press that came out of that was great. I even got a mention in *Autosport*, and in those days karters didn't really get coverage there. Dad also did a good thing with the team and filled the centre-page advert in *Autosport*, so I definitely got noticed because of that.

For Formula Ford I also had Keith Sutton as a sponsor. Keith, of course, had done the press releases for Ayrton Senna and introduced him to the top people in the sport; now we came to an arrangement whereby he would do similar things for me in return for identification on the car. The deal worked really well, and the car looked much better with his branding: Sutton Motorsport logos and an orange chequered flag instead of just plain white bodywork. Our association with Keith really helped a lot in the early days.

I'd known Harald Huysman for a long time. He used to race for Eddie Jordan and later drove a Porsche sponsored by Hydro Aluminium. I did the photographic deal for that. When Harald first started working with Jenson he remembered that I'd done all of Ayrton's PR in the early days, and then Mauricio Gugelmin's, and a few others. He approached me at the GP at Imola in 1998 and gave me the Harald talk about Jenson, that he was going to be the Next Big Thing. Would I like to put some money up? Do some photography? Some PR? I said first of all that I'd like to meet Jenson, so he and his dad came to our office in Towcester a week later. I showed them how our operation worked and we tossed some ideas about, how we could work together. I liked them both, and we struck a deal. I wouldn't put any money in, but we would get him publicity. They had a white car with no logos on it, so they said we could put Sutton Motorsport logos all over it and on Jenson's overalls and helmet in return for the photography, PR and promotion.

When I did Senna we used to send out twenty press

releases, ten to the team owners and ten to the press. Now, twenty years on, it was two hundred as we'd built up quite a network of magazines and clients worldwide. We were able to do a lot more for Jenson than we'd done for Ayrton. We set up his own website and sent out these releases after each Formula Ford race. One of our employees, Jude Martindale, had a keen interest in motorsport, so we let her handle it all.

The first race we had all the stickers ready was Donington, where the car looked great and Haywood's operation was just so professional. For me it was just like going back in time, because in my early days I used to cover all the Formula Ford races. Jenson was third that day, so we were well chuffed.

Keith Sutton, Sutton Motorsport Images

I had developed great relationships with the people at Haywood Racing. Jim Warren is a good bloke. And Puddy, Jesus! What a guy! We all got on really well. Derek was quick, and he was a good team-mate to have. He was experienced, and good competition. I couldn't have wished for anyone better. In the brief time he was with the team, Richard Antinucci was also very quick. For the first part of the season the Mygale had the edge over the Van Diemen, and in the middle they were about the same, but as the season wore on Van Diemen's car gradually got better and better. We were still winning races with our Mygales, but towards the end of the year it got more and more difficult, so every race I won became more pleasurable because the opposition was getting quicker and quicker.

The more races Jenson won that year, the more I was convinced I could tell people in F1 about him. And that's what I started doing in May 1998. All the daily national

newspaper journalists were kept informed, and we began working on a brochure ready to raise the funding for a Formula Three budget the following year. And from August onwards we began getting more features in foreign magazines and I got Jenson a column in Japan, in another magazine called *Autosport*. Suddenly there were all these readers remembering about the work we'd done with Senna, now reading about this new guy who was coming up. They were the first people to know about him, so his following over there began to grow.

Keith Sutton

On 19 September 1998 I won the TOCA Slick 50 Formula Ford Championship at the first attempt, but the big deal as far as I was concerned was winning the Formula Ford Festival (renamed the World Cup) at the end of the season, which was certainly the most satisfying win of my career to that point. In between those two races came the finale for the Euroseries, which ran in parallel to the British series. Derek and I were very competitive in that, too. I was second to Craig Murray in the first round, at Paul Ricard, after taking pole, then at Spa I was slipstreaming Derek for the lead when he made a small mistake, I hooked a wet kerb and spun while trying to avoid him. I recovered to finish fifth. I won at Hockenheim, when I was fastest in the rain, so it came down to a fight between the two of us for the title at Brands Hatch in mid-October.

I had that championship easily in my pocket. All I had to do was finish in front of Derek, and I was soon running in second place behind Ricardo van der Ende, with Derek in sixth or seventh. It could have been an easy championship win, but I couldn't stand being in second behind a car that was quite a bit slower. On the second or third lap, going into Clearways, the last corner, I went for the lead down the inside. Ricardo tried to defend his position, I hit his car at the wrong angle, the wheels got caught up and we ended up in the barriers. All Derek had to do after that was finish in the top three. He went on to win the race and the title. I was runner-up.

It was frustrating to lose the Euroseries in such a way. It was my mistake completely, 100 per cent. I was annoyed with myself for jeopardizing a title in such a fashion. I sat on the sidelines, watching and thinking, 'Oh my God, what did I do?' Van der Ende came up and said, 'What was that for? All you had to do was finish behind me and it would have been easy for you.' But it's so difficult to race like that. It was nothing compared to the Festival win on 25 October, though, so it didn't really matter.

The Festival is the World Championship of Formula Ford, and in testing the Van Diemens were always quicker than us. Always. I missed most of the testing because I was doing the nomination tests for the *Autosport* Awards, and then one of the days was rained off. When it got to qualifying for the race, they were quicker again. Their cars just seemed to be working better in the conditions, and for Brands they'd had a special tweak. I qualified third for the final, with the two works Van Diemens of Daniel Wheldon and Marcus Ambrose ahead of me. In the race itself, the three of us managed to get clear of the pack and were swapping positions all the time. With two laps to go, I pulled exactly the same move on Ambrose that I'd tried on van der Ende, which some people said was quite naughty, but this time it came off for me. Ambrose didn't try to turn in like van der Ende had, although our wheels were interlocked all through the corner. On the exit we just touched, and he slid into the gravel, but I stayed on. So it didn't work at the Euroseries but it did at the Festival, and I know which one I'd rather have won. Wheldon came on strong over those final laps, but I held him off to win by a tiny margin.

To take that race under such circumstances was really satisfying. And to win it in the last two laps made it very special. That evening we all celebrated in the Kentagon, the big bar at Brands, and after a few bevvies everyone was singing Tina Turner's 'Simply The Best' together on stage, which was the perfect ending to a great day.

It was a fascinating season, full of new experiences. Besides a trip to Barcelona late in April to meet team owners at the Spanish Grand Prix, Keith Sutton had also organized for me to meet Norbert Haug, the sporting director of Mercedes, during a sportscar race at Donington, and to have a trip round the Williams factory in June. That was where I learned just how much Frank's son, Jonathan, who was behind the invitation, follows karting and the progress of young drivers. I didn't meet Frank that day because he was off at a test watching Bruno Junqueira, but in any case Johnnie probably knows more about upcoming drivers than anyone else in Formula One. Keith also got me a personal deal with Sony PlayStation, and I wore one of their caps. He did a lot behind the scenes for me in 1998. For 2000, Sutton Motorsports' Jude Martindale moved over to run Jenson Racing, the company that looks after my day-to-day affairs. She has the unenviable job of keeping tabs on my diary and organizing my working life for me. She does a great job, considering how difficult I can be!

I had done well enough on the track in 1998 to get a nomination for the BRDC McLaren *Autosport* Young Driver Award at the end of the season. This is the most prestigious award any young racer can aspire to, and as its name implies it's a jointly sponsored exercise created by the McLaren F1 team, the British Racing Drivers' Club and *Autosport*, the weekly motorsport Bible. In other words, it's run by heavy-hitting people who know what they are talking about. Just getting a nomination is a really big deal, a seal of approval on your racing performances. Imagine a sort of junior motor-racing Oscars, and that's pretty much what it represents in our sport. Any young driver who gets nominated can take that nomination to the bank as far as looking for sponsorship is concerned, because it means he has really achieved something.

But the guy who wins . . . he gets an even bigger slice of cake, because part of the winner's package is a test in a McLaren Formula One car. It's a sensational prize.

After our nominations we had to participate in a series of tests at Silverstone. First of all we drove one of the Silverstone Racing School's Lotus Elises. Then we had a drive in a Formula Three car, Alan Docking Racing's Dallara Mugen-Honda, and a Nissan Primera touring car. I really enjoyed that! When I did my run it was soaking wet, the circuit was flooded. You wouldn't have driven it in a Formula One car. They subsequently decided that they wanted to do it again in the dry, so we had to go back a second time. We also had to do a series of videoed interviews, which was interesting but nerve-racking. I can't remember what I said, I just told the truth and that was it. BRDC secretary John Fitzpatrick just sat you down and asked you why you wanted the award, what you wanted in your career and what you'd get out of the award were you given it. I just thought, 'Oh my God! Just let me drive the cars and see what happens!' Then we had some media-type interviews and a fitness test, although I don't think these were the most important aspects; that was driving the Formula Three car. It was all good fun and I really enjoyed it. I think the other guys who were there with me enjoyed it too.

The awards ceremony itself was almost as glitzy as the Oscars, and that year it was held on Sunday, 6 December at the Grosvenor House Hotel on Park Lane. The location merely added to the sense of occasion, and raised all of our pulse rates accordingly. I can honestly say that I was far more nervous as the evening progressed, waiting for the final outcome, than ever I was during the tests or sitting on the grid prior to the start of a race. It was a strange evening. People always say, 'Oh, you must have known!' But believe me, you don't have a clue. We certainly didn't. You have some idea who your main opposition is, however, and I thought mine was Matt Davies, another karting graduate and a quick little driver. I thought he and I had done the best job in 1998, and he seemed very quick in his Formula Three car. But then again he had more experience, and I think they considered that as well.

We were all stood backstage. It was a tense moment. Past winners included David Coulthard and Dario Franchitti, so that gives you some idea of where this prestigious award can lead you. Old friends such as fellow racer Doug Bell were there, and everyone kept telling me that I'd won it easily. I kept thinking, 'Oh no. If I don't get it now this is going to be really embarrassing.' When eventually we all got up on stage and they announced my name as the winner, it was more a relief than anything else. So many people had been expecting it. It was a great thing to win. I was given a watch, a TAG Heuer, which was a bonus on top of the main award. In fact, I thought that was the best thing about the ceremony – until I remembered that I'd got myself a test in a McLaren Formula One car and a cheque for £50,000 to go towards my next year in racing! It was a great evening.

I remember that evening so well. The ceremony was on the Sunday night and it was all so exciting for us. We were sitting around having coffee beforehand, all wearing our dinner jackets. Hoping Jens was going to win it. And that day's *Independent on Sunday* had a story about Jenson in it and the likelihood that he would be the winner. I still have a copy of it. And we were reading it, and

everyone had a lovely warm feeling inside. It was one of those fairy tales. For that story to begin that day for us, and then for Jenson to go on and win the award as predicted in the paper ... One of the first people to congratulate him afterwards was Damon Hill, one of my heroes. It was just fantastic. One of those evenings you never forget.

John Button

While we were up on the stage, McLaren boss Ron Dennis said something about the possibility of my getting to Formula One in three years, but it honestly didn't register with me until I read it the following Thursday in *Autosport*. I'd never seen my picture up at the front of the magazine before. My God, there were loads of them there, of me smiling in my gold dickie bow-tie, with my blond hair. Loads of quotes from people. It was amazing seeing Ron Dennis saying things about me, good things! At the time it seemed a dream, my being in Formula One in three years' time. The way things worked out, it would take less time than that.

FIVE

CLIMBING THE MOUNTAIN

I'm certainly not the first kart racer who has done well in Formula Ford in his début season, and I won't be the last. But where I was fortunate was in having David Robertson and Harald Huysman behind me. Very few British drivers are able to move seamlessly from the junior category up to the next rung on the ladder, Formula Three. One costs around £100,000 for a season, which is bad enough, but the other is closer to £400,000. The Prime Minister doesn't earn much more than about £100,000 for running the country, so trying to find that sort of money is just ridiculous for most young Brits. And on top of that there's no guarantee, if you find the money, that you will win anything in your first season. You could be looking for twice that sum just to have a second crack at it.

Historically that has always been the problem for British racing drivers, and I'm sure part of the problem is that the majority of industry in this country just doesn't want to invest in nurturing talent. If you look back to the days of Graham Hill, Jim Clark, John

Surtees, Jackie Stewart, James Hunt, Nigel Mansell or Damon Hill, none of them received huge backing in their struggle to make it. All of them succeeded in spite of all the obstacles put in their way, rather than via the sort of driver assistance schemes that foreign companies, such as Elf in France in the 1960s and 1970s, created as a means of bringing on the champions of the future. It's something I've always felt strongly about. Britain is crying out for some sort of properly funded scholarship scheme capable of helping the right drivers into the right seats all the way through their careers.

I was able to bypass a great deal of the end-of-season blues many drivers suffer as they wonder what the hell they'll be driving in the year to come, or even if they'll be driving at all. By October 1998 I was able to look ahead to what I would be doing in Formula Three the following season.

At the end of the 1998 season I had three Formula Three tests. I ran for BSR at Croix-en-Ternois in France, then at Le Mans the next day for Graf Racing. Both wanted me to race for them in Macau, but I felt that would be too much, too soon. Then I went to Magny-Cours with Promatecme, another top Formula Three team, run by Frenchman Serge Saulnier.

I was getting a bit concerned that it was getting late to organize a Formula Three deal for Jenson for 1999, so I took him along to the final meeting of the year to introduce him to various people I knew. My dad and I met up with Jenson and John, and it was the first Formula Three meeting I'd been to in years. I knew Serge Saulnier of Promatecme because they were based at Silverstone and all the guys used to come and order prints from us at the end of the year. Serge is a nice, straightforward bloke, no messing.

I went to the motorhome and saw Serge and Tim

Jackson of Renault UK. Tim asked if I could come back after the race. It turned out it would have been better not to have talked afterwards because in the meantime Renault and Enrique Bernoldi lost the British Formula Three Championship in that race so Tim was a little pre-occupied. But we sat down with him, showed him the brochure and gave him the full spiel. Tim was very honest and told us that Renault had a policy of employing only drivers who'd come from Renault's feeder champion-ships, but he told us to keep in touch.

We went away a bit disappointed, but just as they were packing away all the equipment I saw Serge and managed to introduce him to Jenson. They chatted politely for a few minutes, then Jenson and John left for Frome. I kept talking to Serge and gave him the brochure and the treatment. We chatted for half an hour, and I was really going for it! In the end he turned round and said, 'OK, Keith. I'll take a punt on it and give him a test at Magny-Cours.' I looked at him and just thought, 'Bloody hell, that was easy!' And straight after he'd won the *Autosport* Award, Jenson went down to Magny-Cours to do the test.

Keith Sutton, Sutton Motorsport Images

The very fact that I got the Promatecme chance was a tribute to the team around me including Mygale, who also put in a good word for me. Harald had called Serge Saulnier at around the same time as Keith had introduced me to him. He and Harald had a connection from Harald's Formula Three days, and later, when Promatecme tested a Norwegian driver, Tommy Rustaad, on Renault's behalf in 1995. Mygale, the chassis manufacturers, had also said some nice words about me and recommended that Serge should test me. At the same time, David was busy talking again to Tim Jackson, so we were all pushing every which way.

I was still on cloud nine after the *Autosport* Awards when I went down to Magny-Cours, not far from the famous Le Mans track in France, to try out the Dallara-Renault on 5 November. I didn't know the circuit, and when I got there I found out that I was the only driver to try the car who did not have some sort of prior affiliation with Renault. Among those who had driven it a few days earlier was Aluizio Coelho, a very highly rated Brazilian who was the reigning champion of Formula Renault.

On the morning of the test the weather was pretty foul. The track was wet and we had to wait for the fog to lift. I managed fewer than ten laps before the lunch break.

After five laps Serge came to me and said, 'Has Jenson never driven at Magny-Cours?' Well, Serge knows the place like the back of his own hand, and he said he was very impressed with the accuracy of Jenson's lines. He'd gone out on the circuit to watch, and said, 'He picks up tracks very nicely, and his gearshifting is beautiful.' By the time Jenson had done ten laps, Saulnier was smiling. He was very enthusiastic through lunch.

Harald Huysman

When the test resumed after lunch the track had dried out, and I did another ten laps. The whole thing just flowed and I really enjoyed myself. The times were quick, and I felt as if I'd been driving Formula Three cars all my career. But when I came into the pits Serge told me I could get out of the car. I thought, 'What have I done?' He said he'd seen enough, and then went off to call Tim Jackson at Renault UK to say I should get the drive. It was quite funny, seeing as all the Frenchies, guys with affiliations with Renault, were there. Serge said he'd made his decision. 'You can keep testing or you can stop,' he told me. That's what he said! And I just sat there thinking, 'Oh my God! This is possibly the best drive I could have in Formula Three!'

That morning, while we waited for the fog to lift, I had sat for forty-five minutes with Serge in his car, talking about Jenson's career. And I'd asked him how long it might be before they took any sort of decision about the drivers he would run in the British Formula Three Championship in 1999. This is the most prestigious single-seater champion-ship in the UK, and is also rated very highly in Europe, even though other countries also have their own series. It's the championship that gave the world Nelson Piquet and Ayrton Senna, or Martin Brundle and David Coulthard. So Serge wasn't going to rush into things. He said it would probably be five weeks or so before he made any decision.

After Jenson had completed his twentieth lap of the day, Serge came down off the pit wall and into the garage and sat down beside me. 'Well, if you want it, the drive is yours,' he said. I asked, 'What about the five weeks, and Renault UK?' And he told me, 'From what I have seen today, Jenson is very, very special. I have been in Formula Three for many years and I cannot remember when I last saw something like this.'

Harald Huysman

So it was a bloody good test. We kept Serge's offer quiet to begin with, until Renault was ready to make its official announcement. Serge did us a very good deal, while Promatecme's sponsor Fina personally backed me to the tune of £150,000.

So there I was, my nineteenth birthday approaching, only a year out of karts, a fully fledged professional racing driver with a free works Renault drive in Formula Three. We massaged a further deal with Marlboro, and suddenly we had a full budget and were ready to go racing. For me it was a dream come true. I guess I was lucky that, after those initial days trying to find a Formula Ford budget, I never again had to worry about looking for the money for my racing. That's usually the situation enjoyed by overseas drivers who come to Britain, especially the Brazilians, who tend to have the full funding that allows them to focus 100 per cent on their racing, but not for British drivers. I think I appreciate more now than I did then just what that meant to my career. It was just a fabulous opportunity.

Looking back, things happened too quickly. My first Formula Three race was at Donington Park in Leicestershire on 21 March, and I put the car on pole position in the wet. I really hadn't expected that. Promatecme was a damn good team with a lot of experience, but I was a rookie and so was my new team-mate, Aluizio Coelho, and we were up against some pretty strong opposition. People have likened the 1999 season to 1978, when Englishman Derek Warwick fought against Brazilian Nelson Piquet, or 1983, when Martin Brundle battled Ayrton Senna. This time the fight was going to be between Luciano Burti, from Senna's home town of São Paulo, and twenty-one-year-old Marc Hynes, both of whom had raced in the series the previous season. Burti was staying with the crack Paul Stewart Racing team, which was recognized as the place to be, while Hynes had left Promatecme after a disappointing 1998 to join Manor Motorsport. Manor was a rookie team, but they had won the Formula Renault title with Hynes in 1997. Manor's proprietor, John Booth, was a no-nonsense former racer who knew every nook and cranny of the game.

So, as I said, I was surprised to be on pole. And delighted when I finished second behind Marc in the race, ahead of Luciano. A week later at Silverstone I qualified fourth and finished sixth. Marc won again. Third time out, at Thruxton on 11 April, I was second on the grid and won my first Formula Three race. It was like a fairy tale. I felt as though I was walking on air – until we got to Brands Hatch. That was a double-header meeting, with two races in one day. I qualified fourth and fifth for them and finished eighth and seventh. The bubble had burst!

Throughout the season we were faced with a very difficult problem. Hynes and Burti were running an identical car, but where mine was powered by a Renault engine theirs had the Mugen-Honda, which was more powerful. Renault had recently changed their engine supplier from Renault Sport to Sodemo, and it took a while for things to settle down. Before they did we had a serious straight-line speed problem. It wasn't until the end of the year that we started to get close to the Mugen-Hondas, but usually when we closed on them they could find a little extra. We couldn't be critical about the power unit because we were the official Renault team. In any case, it's not my style to criticize things publicly when you're trying to work together. Outside the team a lot of people drew the distinction between the two engines when they were talking or writing about us, but for my part, I had to take responsibility for the problems I was contributing to the team in the form of my complete inexperience in terms of setting up this sort of car.

I got my head back into the right gear at Oulton Park in Cheshire in May, where I qualified second and finished fifth, and followed that up in June with a third fastest practice time and my first failure to finish, after the throttle stuck open. I was third on the grid again at Brands Hatch later that month, and finished sixth.

I was pleased with my qualifying performances, but less happy about my race results. Since Thruxton, Luciano had won twice and Marc once, and the other two races had gone to the Indian driver Narain Karthikeyan.

When I was racing in Formula Three one of the big-deal races was the supporting event at the British GP. It was the perfect opportunity to showcase yourself to the Formula One team owners. After practice on Thursday for the 10 July race I took provisional pole position, which was very pleasing. I deliberately sat in the pit lane for about ten minutes because I didn't want to waste my time while others cleared away the loose stuff on the track surface. When I did go out I put in a fastest time straight away. Burti beat it later, but even as he was doing that I was on a quicker lap still and won provisional pole back almost before the computers could register the time. Because of that I got some press interviews when I managed to get into the Formula One paddock later on, all of which was good experience.

In the end Marc started on pole, but I made a better start and led as far as Vale. Some people were quick to say that it was the greater horsepower of the Mugen-Honda that allowed Marc to pull out and slip ahead of me going into Club Corner, but by then Sodemo had come up with some important modifications to the engines and they were a lot stronger. No, that one was down to me. My mistake. I just had more to learn about running an opening lap on cold tyres, and Marc got a better exit from Stowe corner and dragged by me. I shouldn't have left him a gap. I kept the pressure on him throughout the race and set the fastest lap, but Marc's a good driver and he didn't make any mistakes, so I finished second. Luciano was third.

A fortnight later at Snetterton in Norfolk fourth place on the grid became eleventh after I had spun trying to pass Luciano for the lead and had to fight back up from last place. Then came the prestigious

Marlboro Masters at Zandvoort in Holland. The Marlboro Masters is not part of any championship, but like Macau is one of the jewels in the category's crown. I had problems all through qualifying and was only in the mid-field on the grid, but things got better during the race and I managed to hack up to finish fifth. In the circumstances I was quite pleased with that, but I was getting frustrated. I had long since abandoned ideas of a maiden season title run; instead, we were going for individual race wins. In August I went back to Pembrey, where I had had that first test in a Formula Three car for Carlin, for another double-header race. I was second on the grid for the first one to the Danish driver Kristian Kolby, and he led me home by ten seconds, but I set the fastest lap. I had been leading by a large margin when I was given a stop and go penalty for creeping at the start. Everyone did it but mine was the car everyone was watching. I fell to fifth as I served the penalty, but climbed up to second by the finish. The second race was much better for me. I started from pole position and won, beating Matt Davies and Kolby and again setting the fastest lap. I felt elated, especially as the two results moved me ahead of Karthikeyan and up into third place in the championship behind Burti and Hynes.

Donington in September brought another front-row start and a second place, but I should have won there. I almost stalled on the grid, so Burti was able to come round me into second place, and I lost time in the opening lap while I figured out where to repass him. He left the door open at the last corner and I was able to come from a long way back to slip inside him, but by then Marc had gone.

Then came Spa, the British series' only visit to a foreign circuit. I love Spa, with the fabulous challenge of its uphill Eau Rouge corner, and I felt that all Sodemo's work on our Renault engine was finally beginning to pay off. I was delighted to outpace both Burti and Hynes to take pole position. It was a real confidence booster. I knew that both of them would have to be a bit careful in the race because they were fighting for the championship, but I also knew that if either of them beat me into La Source I now had the package to overtake them.

The start worked out really well, and by the end of the first lap I had a lead of a second and a half, but then the safety car came out because there had been a shunt on the start line. We all closed up again. Then my car began to bottom out at Eau Rouge on its now cold tyres. You reach motor racing's most fantastic corner by speeding downhill from the La Source hairpin at the start of the lap. At maximum speed, around 160mph, you steer slightly left on entry. Then the road curves right in a really steep climb – far steeper in reality than it looks on television – before turning sharply left then flicking right on the long climb up the straight at Raidillon and on to Les Combes at the top of the climb. Eau Rouge is not the place where you want the bottom of the car touching the track. Your speed through Eau Rouge determines your speed on the ensuing straight. In practice I'd been going through Eau Rouge flat with no lift on the throttle, but now I was nowhere near as quick. At the restart Marc and Luciano came by me on the climb to Les Combes. I just had to hold on and hope that nobody else came by, but they did. My team-mate Coelho did the same. I managed to repass him going into La Source, but as I outbraked him Kolby got a run at both of us and took me for third place after Eau Rouge. It was a mega disappointment after taking pole, but I just had to wait until my fuel load lightened and the floor of the car stopped touching the track at Eau Rouge. By the time that happened I was forced to play catch-up, and of course I'd run out of time. Luciano beat Marc by a second, but I was another five places further back, still chasing Kolby.

Later I was down to do the 24-hour touring car race at Spa in a Team Rafanelli BMW, with David Saelens and Tomas Enge as team-mates. I didn't get to race as we had fuel problems, but it was the most exhilarating experience in my career to date, driving the car in qualifying in the dark. As I shifted from fifth to fourth gear at Eau Rouge flames would shoot out of the exhaust, just like the car was on fire.

Silverstone in October brought me my third and final Formula Three victory. I was fascinated to see how Luciano and Marc would handle the start. They collided, letting me slip into second behind Matt Davies. I outbraked him at Abbey on the ninth lap, and set the fastest lap on my way home. Promatecme gave me a top-of-the-podium car that day, and it felt really good to avenge the disappointments of Spa.

In the finale at Thruxton on 17 October I was out to win again, but it all went wrong for me on the first lap. I started fourth on the grid but was elbowed to seventh by the end of lap one as Warren Hughes slipped ahead of Marc and me. I then got off line and lost more places. Things improved for a while after that – I overtook Tim Spouge at the Complex on lap four, then got Hynes there a lap later, which was highly satisfying – but at the chicane after eight laps I tangled with Andrew Kirkcaldy, whose car was in imminent danger of retiring with an engine fault. That was the end for me.

The British Formula Three Championship was over, and I had finished third. Marc Hynes was the deserving champion with 213 points to Luciano Burti's 209, and I had 168. In my seventeen starts I was on the front row eight times and on pole three times, and I notched up seven podium finishes, three victories and four fastest laps. But the season wasn't quite over. It ended with a brace of non-championship races in the Pacific Rim, the first on the streets of Macau, the other in Korea. Both were won by fellow Englishman Darren Manning in a Dallara with an awesome Toyota motor, but I was second in each race and damn nearly caught him for the win in Korea when he backed off too much as he approached the line. I got within a second of him.

Macau is one mega place. It used to be a Portuguese colony but is now part of China again. The night life was just extraordinary, to say the least! I had a swell time there, over and above the racing.

Looking back over my season, I remembered and was intrigued by a comment of Serge's made at Silverstone in October: he said that when I'm leading I do the perfect job. I thought my results were good, for a first season, but if someone had asked me mid-season whether I was disappointed, I'd have said yes. There was a lot to take into consideration. I had my fair share of highs and lows – some might say more than my fair share. It was a high when I won at Thruxton in only my third Formula Three race, but we weren't expecting that, and maybe it gave us a problem because after it expectations were perhaps too high. And I didn't expect pole for my first race. That's not to say that I thought I'd make a slow start to the season, but that pole and then the ensuing second place in my first race was too much, too soon. Maybe it made everyone relax a little bit too much, maybe we didn't work on the car so much, maybe we should have done more testing . . .

Brands Hatch in April was the real low point. It came at a time when I had some good results in the bank, but my performance in that double-header was not good. I stalled the car on the grid, for a start. OK, it was confusing with yellow flags waving everywhere, but I shouldn't have done that. I'd never done that before. My own feelings were at a lower ebb because I'd won the Formula Ford Festival there the year before, so not doing so well in a Formula Three car wasn't great. It really knocked my confidence, and fast driving is all about confidence. I have to win as a racing driver, all the time, and when it didn't happen at Brands I just had to pick myself up and sort myself out.

I may look angelic here, but I'm sure my hyperactive nature caused Dad more than a few anxious moments in my childhood. Button Family

All suited up at the age of seven, I was soon tearing around on my 50cc Yamaha motorbike. Button Family

ABOVE: The minute Dad offered me a chance to race my Cadet kart, I grabbed it. Here I'm at Clay Pigeon in Somerset, aged eight. Button Family

ABOVE: Dad waits with me on the grid for a 1989 Cadet race, with Anthony Davidson (6) and Jay Howard (66) for company. This is the helmet that would later inspire the Italians to regard me as something of a devil. Button Family

LEFT: Just to prove that I did sometimes go to school ... Button Family

Team Rambo ran with Astra sponsorship in 1994, hence the pink overalls. This is me in the Margutti Trophy race at Parma in Italy, my first big outing abroad. Button Family

The first time I met Jos Verstappen was during the Formula A World Championship meeting in 1995, when I was competing with Paul Lemmens's GKS team. In Brazil in 2000 I would overtake him to claim my first ever World Championship point in my second Grand Prix. Button Family

Besides becoming the first Englishman ever to win the European Super A Karting Championship in 1997, I also won the Senna Memorial Cup after fighting from 18th to second in the World Championship at Suzuka in my GKS Tecno Rotax.

Caro/Sutton Motorsport Images

In April 1998 I made a trip to the Spanish GP at Barcelona, where I was able to meet F1 powerbrokers such as Bernie Ecclestone. Sutton Motorsport Images

BELOW LEFT: I wouldn't have got so far without the help at key stages of people such as my former managers Harald Huysman and David Robertson (*far left* and *left*) and photographer Keith Sutton (*right*). Sutton Motorsport Images

BELOW RIGHT: Dad and I can hardly believe it as we celebrate my success in the BRDC McLaren Autosport Young Driver Awards at the Grosvenor House Hotel in December 1998. It has yet to sink in fully that part of my prize is a test drive in a McLaren F1 car.

Bearing allegiance to my supporters, I had a wonderful season in Formula Ford in 1998, which culminated in title success first time out in the Slick 50 Championship. Sutton Motorsport Images

Among the guys I raced against in 1998 were my Haywood Racing Mygale team-mate Derek Hayes (*left*) and my old karting friend and rival Tom Sisley (*right*). Sutton Motorsport Images

TOP LEFT: Serge Saulnier gave me a great chance to race for his Team Promatecme operation in Formula Three in 1999, with backing from Renault, Fina and Marlboro. I won three races, and suddenly found myself heading for Formula One a lot sooner than I had expected.

BOTTOM LEFT: In November 1999 I finally got my first taste of Formula One when I tested this McLaren-Mercedes at Silverstone as part of my prize for winning the BRDC McLaren Autosport Young Driver Award the previous year. LAT

TOP RIGHT: Four-time World Champion Alain Prost was one of the first people to show serious interest in me as a Formula One driver.
Batchelor/Sutton Motorsport Images

MIDDLE RIGHT: I loved driving Alain's AP03 at Barcelona in December 1999, and my performance there really started the ball rolling.
Batchelor/Sutton Motorsport Images

BOTTOM RIGHT: There was a lot of tension underlying my fight with Bruno Junqueira for the second seat at BMW Williams for 2000, but driving the interim car in Jerez and Barcelona was a fantastic experience that I thoroughly enjoyed.
Bearne/Sutton Motorsport Images

LEFT: Right from the moment I first met him during my trip to the Spanish GP in 1998, I hit it off with Sir Frank Williams, a man for whom I have immense respect. Sutton Motorsport Images

BELOW: This is the shunt that a lot of people had been predicting, on Saturday morning of the Australian GP in 2000, my Formula One début. It was one of the few times I've really damaged a racing car. LAT

BELOW: My engineer Tim Preston (*second from left*) was great company during my maiden year of Formula One. My friend and physio Hogne Rorvik is holding the umbrella. Rose/Sutton Motorsport Images

We did a lot of work as a team after that. When we went to Croft near Darlington in County Durham in June it was great. I didn't finish because the throttle stuck open, but what was important there was the speed and the set-up. The boys at Promatecme did a really good job, and we went off to the British GP meeting on a real high. We had done a lot of testing and my starts were sorted out, besides which we knew there would be a good crowd at Silverstone and I always go best in front of a big crowd. I think I got used to that the previous year in Formula Ford, where we were with the touring cars for every race and they attracted good crowds. Even though I didn't win that race I tried bloody hard to, and I think I gained some respect that weekend. Some people referred to it as a rebirth, but really we'd passed the turning point of the season when we decided to forget about the championship and just go for wins.

The transition from Formula Ford to Formula Three isn't really all that easy. When you first get into a Formula Three car it feels great, only a touch strange, because the car is much longer than a Formula Ford and in the corners the weight is much further away from you. That's difficult to try to explain, but what I mean is that it's hard to feel the balance of the car as you get used to the effect of downforce at different speeds. You can be reasonably quick straight away in a Formula Three car, but it's learning to get those extra half-seconds that's the secret, and in order to find them you have to drive constantly on the edge. It takes time to master it.

After the second Brands race the team and I worked well and everything really came together. I was getting to know the car. By that stage I could feel the effects of changing the aerodynamics, whereas before I couldn't feel anything. As a result I started making some good input on set-up. I guess I was learning Formula Three, and this was important for us. Neither Aluizio nor I had any previous Formula Three experience to speak of at the beginning of the year, unlike Marc and Luciano, both of whom were driving in their second year. It was important for us to give the right feedback, and that wasn't always easy. If I'd had an experienced team-mate, someone who could have helped to set up the car, it might have been better for me. And vice versa. I don't think I drove a Formula Three car quite like the other drivers did, so that made it difficult to set up. Some of the guys would suggest things for the car that would work with someone who drove it in the classic style, but they wouldn't work for me.

Then there was a lot of hype to begin with, and that was very hard to cope with. But, as a professional, that's just something you have to learn about. It's sometimes hard to put on a smiley public face after a race when you're far from happy. Inside you might really be kicking yourself about something, but outside you have to smile and say the right things. I think I put myself under a fair bit of that sort of pressure, a fact which a lot of people don't appreciate and don't understand about. That's pressure, the racing isn't.

The good results really came in the second half of the year. We all knew we had the straight-line speed problem – the speedtrap information at each track showed that – so taking that into account I think we did bloody well in the end. No-one really knew what we were up against because we didn't openly criticize anything. In the end, I wasn't disappointed that I hadn't been able to win the Formula Three Championship in my first season. I felt I'd done my best and hadn't made many mistakes. Third place in the series, and the first Renault driver, was something to be pleased with. Overall, we did a pretty good job in circumstances that were sometimes far from ideal. Things felt right for a charge at the title in 2000. Little did I know that I was just about to step aboard the rollercoaster that would thrust me into Formula One the best part of two years ahead of Ron Dennis's prediction.

SIX

MY FIRST TASTE OF FORMULA ONE

I was very fortunate as my Formula Three career drew to its conclusion. A lot of people wanted to talk to me. Things began moving quickly as 1999 went into its final quarter, though in retrospect not as fast as they were about to go.

In November I went down to Jerez de la Frontera in Spain for my first chance to test a Formula 3000 car. I did a day with David Sears' crack SuperNova team, and a day and a half with Fortec Motorsport. Both ran the standard Lola-Cosworth cars with their 450bhp V8 engines. To be honest, all of us had hoped that I might be able to avoid the category, and the tests bore out my misgivings about Formula 3000. I thought the car was big and heavy, and a handful to get used to. It felt very different from a Formula Three car and I didn't like it much at all, or the style of driving you needed to get the best from it. The car gave you the feeling that there was so much behind you, pushing you on in the corners under braking. It was really strange. On new tyres the car was great, there was loads of grip, but that was another thing: between old tyres and new tyres there was a massive difference in handling. In Formula Three you don't get that. I would run a lot of laps in the Lola-Cosworth on old tyres and think, 'Yeah, this is the limit, this is the limit.' Then I'd get new tyres and I didn't know where to brake or anything. My lap times, however, were good. I think I ended up sixth quickest, which was OK. But the whole experience endorsed my view that I had to avoid the category if at all possible, though of course I would have raced in it had there been nothing else available.

At the end of April 1998 Harald and I had made the trip out to the Spanish Grand Prix at Barcelona, where Keith had teed up some meetings and sorted me out a pit pass. It was an important thing to do, and an ideal opportunity for me to meet some of the leading team owners, the men who would matter most as my career developed. It was a fascinating experience. I met Bernie Ecclestone for the first time, which was good because I was able to thank him for allowing Keith to get a pass for me. In fact he gave me a fair bit of his time, which I thought was very good of him, given the schedule he has at races. I also met Sir Frank Williams and Patrick Head, McLaren chief Ron Dennis, Jordan owner Eddie Jordan, Tom Walkinshaw at Arrows, and Jackie and Paul Stewart. And a few journalists.

You hear so much about Formula One when you're racing in other categories, and here I was, right at the heart of it. But at the same time it wasn't one of those experiences that overawes you. I talked to a lot of people that weekend and was able to form a lot of impressions and opinions, about people and about situations. All the team owners I talked to were polite and I was grateful for their time and advice. I was quite surprised that they went to the trouble on a race weekend. Of all the people I met there, though, the one I liked the best was Frank Williams. He is a great guy. ('Respect!' as

Ali G would say.) Frank was interested in what I had been doing and seemed to know quite a lot about me, and genuinely wanted to know what my views were on certain things. I felt as though he was talking to me, not at me. We just seemed to click. Overall, some of the advice I received was extremely helpful, some was more self-serving, designed to benefit the giver's own ends. But it was a great weekend. My resolve to get to Formula One didn't necessarily need strengthening, but now I had a better idea of what it was all about. Perhaps most importantly of all, I didn't see anything I thought I wouldn't be able to handle. I'd seen Formula One at first hand, close up, and I felt it was an environment in which I could make myself comfortable.

At the same time Keith was, as ever, busy on my behalf. He felt that the timing was absolutely right to push things on the publicity side, because Damon Hill was retiring at the end of that season and Johnny Herbert wasn't going to stick around much longer. Keith was telling all the Fleet Street journalists that they should get behind me because pretty soon they were going to need a new British driver. It's obviously better for them that the country has a Brit to get behind so that they can maintain their sports editors' interest in the sport. It's always better when there's a home boy in the field.

To their credit, they responded brilliantly. Suddenly I found myself the subject of features in all the leading nationals – the *Daily Telegraph*, the *Daily Mail*, the *Sun*, the *Daily Express*, the *Independent on Sunday* – even though I was still racing in Formula Ford at the time. It was fantastic coverage for me. The funny thing was that all the other drivers just couldn't figure it out. They were getting out-psyched because I was getting all this publicity. 'Why is this other guy getting all the stories?' they were asking themselves. 'He isn't the only one who's winning.' It was like being inside a great big snowball that was just getting bigger and bigger as it rolled down the hill.

That November at Silverstone I got my first chance to see Formula One from another angle – from the cockpit of a McLaren, part of my prize for being chosen as the BRDC McLaren *Autosport* Young Driver of the year. Unfortunately, the weather did its best to spoil the occasion. We used the National circuit at Silverstone and the track was wet but drying. The team didn't want to use dry-weather tyres, probably because it was risky in the circumstances, so I could only do a handful of timed laps before the wet-weather tyres would be destroyed. I did one ten-lap stint, then came in. But I didn't do more than eight of my next ten laps. I came into the pits and told them there was no use carrying on. I wasn't going to learn anything and there was no use driving a car like that with the tyres chunking away. It wasn't helping anyone. They said fine, and that was it. We went through the data, and that was the end of it, really. A bit of an anti-climax, though I don't mean any disrespect when I say that. It was a wonderful opportunity.

The test was wet, but the track was drying. It wasn't a good time for him to be running, to be honest. He was impressive, but not for what he did in the car so much as the way he handled himself. When I reported back to Martin Whitmarsh [managing director of McLaren International] I told him that I couldn't say what sort of a driver he was, but the guy handled himself incredibly well just the way he approached it, the way he drove the car. He used the radio, it just seemed natural to him; he told us what he was doing all the time. The track was drying, the tyres were falling apart, and he told us he was going to slow down, do one slow lap and then go and do one more quick one. And then, the most impressive thing really, was that he didn't use all his laps up. He said, 'No, I'm wasting my time. The tyres are not in good enough

condition, I'm going to call it a day.' We were running Jenson and Andrew Kirkcaldy as *Autosport* prize winners, and he was impressive considering that they only got two ten-lap runs each.

Davy Ryan, team manager, McLaren

I'd used a radio in Formula Three, although not very much, just in the pits. I certainly didn't think as I slotted myself into the car, 'Oh, I'd better do this and that to impress them.' I just drove it the way I thought best. The funny thing was that the radio button was a latch. You pushed it on and it stayed on for a certain amount of time. The light for it was so bright I was almost blinded driving down the straight. I had a clear visor on because it was wet, and there was this big blue light on the dashboard!

The most noticeable difference with a Formula One car – apart from the speed and the phenomenal braking, obviously – was the amount of movement you get over bumps. The car squirmed. The degree of movement was unbelievable. The other thing was how quickly you could go through the gearbox with the semi-automatic change. Through Copse I could still feel that the g force was greater than anything I'd ever experienced, even in the wet, but I felt so comfortable with it. For the first three laps I couldn't stop laughing! The McLaren was obviously a very good car, just about the best I could have driven in at that time. I could get it oversteering, but it was only a gradual oversteer. Sometimes you get a car that's very snappy, but that one was so nice to drive. You could apply the power nice and easily, the car felt softer compared to a Formula Three or 3000 car, and of course back then there was no traction control or anything. You could control the car yourself, and it felt just fantastic. A really, really good feeling.

The hardest thing, just as it proved later when I first drove the

BMW Williams, was pulling smoothly out of the garage. A Formula One clutch was unlike any I'd ever felt, even though I was using a foot clutch. Just like air – there was very little feel it. Normally, of course, you let out the clutch until you feel it beginning to reach its bite point, when the car wants to move; then you apply more throttle and away you go. But on the Williams it was really difficult to feel that bite point; the system gave you such a tiny amount of feedback in that respect. So I stalled it the first time, then pulled out the second time with about 15,000rpm on it to make damn sure it didn't happen again.

So I'd tested a Formula 3000 car in Jerez with mixed feelings, and when December arrived I was still unsure quite what I would be driving in 2000. I knew, at least, that I would continue in Formula Three for a second season with the aim of winning the title or indeed graduate, as it were, to do a season of Formula 3000, and I was confident that something good lay ahead.

We were all surprised when we heard the news that Darren Manning had been offered a Williams test after winning in Macau and Korea. It turned out that Frank Williams knew him personally because he'd previously been up for a Renault touring car test in the days when Williams was still with Renault, and they had kept in touch. In a way we had become victims of our own publicity. Frank had taken the view that if I was supposed to be so special and Darren had beaten me in Macau and Korea, then Darren must be bloody good! Later I found out that Darren's name had in fact replaced mine on the drivers list Frank was keeping.

When I got back from the racing in Korea, Alain Prost invited Dad, Harald and me to go and see him in Paris, and we went out to a nice restaurant. He told me he had been following my career and asked me if I was interested in doing Formula 3000 – the next rung up the ladder, of course, with only Formula One above it. He laid out a contract that marked out a possible route for me over the next few years: maybe another year in Formula Three, maybe some Formula 3000, and for sure Formula One by the third year – but potentially Formula One by the second year.

It was very intriguing because Jarno Trulli had gone to Prost early in his Formula One career, and ever since my karting days I'd tended to follow in Trulli's wheel tracks, so to speak. But I have to say that all of us were dubious about it, because it really depends so much on which team you run with, and Alain's was not at that point seen as one of the top F3000 outfits. Still, it was a pleasant meeting, Alain was charming, and I left feeling very warm inside about the option.

On race day at Monza in September 1999 I'd sat down with Alain Prost in his motorhome to discuss Jenson and go through his career details. Alain had said, 'Five minutes,' as we began, but we finished talking forty-five minutes later. That was bloody good of him. At the same time Serge Saulnier and the guys at Mygale had been speaking to Prost, telling him that he ought to test Jenson. That he was special. As usual, we were trying to attack from several angles.

Alain called me on 10 December, a Friday, and said that the team would be testing in Barcelona the following week. Jean Alesi would have to leave for Paris on the Thursday night, and Alain would be happy to give Jenson a day in the car in a week's time. Were we interested? I told him that we were really honoured, but that I had to clarify something. We were not prepared to sign any sort of commitment before we tested. A lot of people want a young driver to sign an option in such circumstances, so

that if they turn out to be mega quick the team gets its hands on them first. To Alain's eternal credit he did not try to attach the sort of strings others would have been tempted to insist upon. There were no options to be signed. Alain just said it was his pleasure. He was really interested in giving Jenson a chance and would fly down himself to watch the run. That was really, really nice of him. A real gentleman's gesture.

Harald Huysman

Though I was a bit disappointed to miss out on the Williams test, I could at least look confidently towards the future as my girlfriend at the time, Kimberley, and I headed off for a holiday in Mexico. We both just wanted some sun, sea and relaxation now that the season was finally over, and I figured we deserved a break. We went to this plush place in Cancún. The Coral Beach Hotel, with its marble floors, 60 metres of pool and the jacuzzi in the room, was one of the most amazing I've ever stayed in. The perfect place to relax.

We'd been there just six days out of our scheduled two weeks when Dad called. Then David phoned with the same message: Alain Prost had phoned and he wanted to give me a test in one of his Formula One cars in Barcelona the following week. I thought, 'Fantastic!' I was really excited. But David said, 'Don't worry if you want to stay and enjoy your holiday. I know you haven't seen Kim much this year. That's fine, not a problem. I can try and get the test another time.' I was like, 'You what? David, this is a test in a Formula One car that could be a possible test drive next year. Of course I'm gonna come back!'

Kim took it very well. She flew with me from Cancún to Madrid and then down to Barcelona. She was cool with it. Dad flew into

Barcelona from England with my helmet and an old Formula Ford race suit, and Alain flew in on the Thursday evening, 16 December, from Paris. He and the team briefed me fully and told me to take things easy because we had a full day of running. In the garage at the circuit that night we did a rudimentary seat fitting, using somebody else's seat as a basis.

I went to bed that night with excitement welling up inside me, although I felt quite calm about what I had to do. It was a funny feeling: I was really looking forward to the opportunity, but I wasn't feeling at all apprehensive. I knew pretty much what to expect after driving the McLaren, however briefly, and now I was ready to show what I could do.

Jean Alesi had been testing at the Circuit de Catalunya for two days and had set a best time of 1m 24.8s. It had rained on the Wednesday, but Friday, 17 December, dawned clear, with the same weather conditions Jean had enjoyed the previous day. The team sent me out on the same level of fuel he had had, and the tyres he had finished running with. They told me, tongue obviously in cheek as the mileage they mentioned would have been out of the question for a Formula One novice, 'If you do a hundred laps today, don't think about lap times, just learn how to handle a Formula One car and learn the track. It's a very difficult track, so take it easy. If you do a 1m 28s at the end of the day, that's very, very good. If you do a 1m 27.9s that's fantastic. But forget about that.'

It was the perfect environment for my first real Formula One test because everyone in the team was doing their best to make me feel comfortable. I loved driving that car from the moment I sat in it. It was mega. I did five flying laps, and everything just clicked. I felt as though I belonged there, and when I came in I had done a best lap of 1m 26.8s. They sent me out for another six laps, and on the last one I did a 1m 24.4s. Everyone was very excited when I came back into the pits, but at that moment, to be honest, I wasn't sure what all the fuss was about. Until I saw the times.

Everybody had pressured Alain into getting some new drivers, and Jenson's name came up. He was mooted as being a good bet. We got him down to Barcelona, and as far as I'm aware he had never ever driven round it, let alone in a Formula One car. We got him in the car and he was very relaxed about everything. Completely unfazed by doing a pretty major test. Quite professional, the way he wanted the seat properly done. He didn't want a piece of foam, he wanted it properly made, but was quite relaxed about it all.

Actually, it reminded me of the same test I did with another British upcomer in the 1980s, Jason Elliott. When we tested Jason in a Formula 3000 car at Snetterton I heard him go out of the pits and he was just *on* it. He'd never driven an F3000 car before and I heard this car revving up and setting off and coming round Coram and all the other corners at racing speed, and I thought, 'Bloody hell, who is this guy, he's got to slow down!' He was a star who didn't get all the right opportunities.

Jenson went out in the car and did an installation lap – yeah, everything was fine. We told him to watch the brakes and be a little bit careful, and I sent him out on his first run of laps and went back into the garage and was talking to somebody. Other people were testing at the same time, and I heard one car go past using all the road and all the revs, and didn't think anything more of it. I went to the pit wall and asked when Jenson was due round, and somebody said, 'He's already been round. That was him going round then.' And I thought, 'That couldn't have been him,' because the guy was *on* it.

Using the kerbs. People on their first run usually take it easy, but he was inch-perfect on his exit of the corner and his speed on the straight was within 10kph of Jean's the previous day. He came round the next lap, and I thought, 'Bloody hell, was that Jenson going past?' He really *was* on it, drifting round that last corner like he was a regular there. And that's a very quick corner. Within seven or ten laps he was doing Jean's times.

He came into the pits, got out of the car and said, 'Yeah, it's not too bad,' and we were saying, 'Look, you're pretty quick . . .'

He chipped away at his times for the rest of the day and in the end we had one or two problems with the car. He wasn't too comfortable in it, was starting to move around in the seat, and the times tailed off, but had he been fitter and more used to the car we could have got him going quicker still.

It was a shame that the deadlines with the magazines didn't work in Jenson's favour because not too many people got to hear about this straight away. We pushed Alain and said, 'Look, you've got to sign this guy up.' Then it was all too late when the Williams thing came up. But the main thing was that he was unfazed by it all and he was quick. His feedback was good as we made adjustments to the car and he was happier with it. Just like a regular Formula One driver. For me it was incredible. I was well impressed.

Humphrey Corbett, Prost race engineer

It was great to come in after the first run to see everyone smiling and happy with it. I think most Formula One teams are told to keep a straight face when they are testing anyone. It's a strange atmosphere when that happens, but the Prost guys were all smiles. I thought, 'Awesome! That must have been OK then.' We only got thirty laps or so done, though, and then the thing went bang.

Nick Heidfeld was also there that day, and I think my best lap was just two tenths off his time, so to begin with I was very happy to be so close to him because he'd done a lot of Formula 3000 racing and had won the championship that season; he'd also done a lot of testing for McLaren, so he knew his way around, no question. And there I was, already faster than the time Jean Alesi had done in 'my' car, with the same tyres. Jean had done 1m 24.8s, and I did 1m 24.4s.

Then suddenly, at the end of the day when I wasn't running any more because of the mechanical problem on my car, Nick went out again and went a second and a half quicker, or something like that. I thought, 'Jesus Christ, I'm not quick after all!' It was a very disappointing end to a great day.

Of course, at that time I didn't realize he'd put on new tyres, and I didn't really know a great deal about the effects changing a fuel load can have on a Formula One car. A gallon of fuel weighs 12lb, or something like that, so taking fuel out of the car, like we do for qualifying runs, is obviously going to make the car a lot lighter and a lot quicker. But it was a couple of months before I really figured out the full significance of that one. In the meantime I felt a bit detuned, when actually I was entitled to feel quite pleased with myself. You live and you learn.

The timing of that Prost test was funny, because it happened just before Christmas and, as Humphrey mentioned, caught the weekly magazines on the hop. They'd already gone to press with their pre-Christmas issues, and they missed an issue over Christmas, so by the time it was written up early the next year it was old news. That didn't bother me too much, because I knew what I'd achieved in the car. I'd been given a great chance, thanks to Alain, and I thought I'd done a reasonable job.

Sure enough, as I prepared to celebrate the twentieth Christmas of my life, the Formula One jungle drums were beating solidly in the distance and Sir Frank Williams got to know all about my performances in Barcelona.

SEVEN

COPING WITH THE PRESSURE

From the moment I officially became a BMW Williams race driver I was exposed to the world's media. It happened literally within minutes of being told the good news by Frank in Barcelona on 24 January 2000. I barely had time to realize that I had achieved the dream I had been pursuing for years before being shoved through a door on to a stage. My life changed in that moment. It was like that film, *Sliding Doors*: I stepped through from one reality into something completely different. That day I had to confront my new life, and all the media guys there really went to town. Britain hadn't had a new Formula One driver since David Coulthard had come in with Williams Renault after Ayrton Senna's death in May 1994. And there I was, not just a new boy and the youngest of the flock, but the youngest Brit ever to make it to the Big League.

I suppose I should have known I was going to get a bit of press, but when some of the guys brought the British papers out to Barcelona, where we stayed on to do some more testing, and my family faxed some articles over to me, I was just staggered. Most of it was intensely flattering, I suppose – that they should all be so interested in me – but I just didn't know what to say to begin with. As a result I gave them too much, which is maybe a thing I shouldn't have done. Later I learned a bit more, that it was best to be a little bit more circumspect. But I still always do as many interviews as I can and I try to be as happy as I can when doing them, although of course I'm more cautious when it comes to information about my private life and stuff like that.

To be honest, I liked all the attention I got after the launch. I really did. I was still at the stage of my career where I could walk down the street without being recognized, but I think it was good that I remained in Spain for a week after I got chosen for the drive because of all the publicity there was at home. There was just so much stuff flying around about me in England. Somebody said to me recently that the only time Formula One drivers get their faces on the front pages of British quality newspapers is when they've won a race against all expectations or been killed. I was as staggered as everyone else when I saw mine on them even before I'd taken part in my first race.

The Times in particular did me proud. There was a big picture of me on their front page and a cartoon by Pugh of a guy holding out a pit board which read: 'Bedtime at 8.00 p.m.' Very droll. My graduation was even the subject of one of the paper's leaders. It mentioned me in the same breath as Liverpool striker Michael Owen, which was cool, and it said that my arrival was a welcome tonic. Wow!

If I'd walked into a newsagent's back then and seen all of the papers I think I'd have had an even greater shock. I suppose it began to dawn on me then, as I witnessed the sheer weight of publicity that surrounded my arrival in Formula One, just what sort of road I'd set out on. Initially, of course, it was very strange to read all this stuff about me, really strange. But I have to admit that I did get used to it all pretty quickly.

The *Sun* had a piece that was supposedly done by my girlfriend Kim, but she hadn't said half of what was printed under the headline 'BUTTONED UP'. Hadn't heard that one before. (Honest!) Oh boy, what a situation the tabloids can create! To start with, as I said, I gave them a few titbits about my private life that I shouldn't have, and they picked up on that. Then they started to get interested in my family. My mum, Simone, had lots of people coming round to her house and tricking her into talking to them. That made me feel sick, because she has nothing to do with the sport and shouldn't have been hassled like that – and I'm quite an easy-going character. I don't take offence easily.

That experience didn't help my sense of trust with some journalists. The regular tabloid guys in Formula One aren't too bad; it's the ones outside, the so-called general colour piece writers rather than the sports specialists, the ones who often know nothing about motorsport, dart in, scribble something about you and then flit off knowing they won't have to face you again. People warned me to watch out for the tabloids, but to be honest I get on pretty well with most of the journalists in Formula One who work for them. It's not as if they're monsters. They're just ordinary blokes. And it's important to me that I do get on with them, that I have good relationships with them. I take the view that if you speak to them as human beings, they won't have anything too bad to write about you. The specialist racing press guys are fine. They are there primarily because they love and understand the sport.

You have to give the media as much as you can, within reason. They like it if you spend time with them. Most drivers do their twenty or thirty minutes or whatever and then leave, whereas I try to spend a little bit of extra time with them, even if I'm just talking about nothing. Things completely away from Formula One. If you take the time to get to know them I think they respect you a little bit more. Despite all the crap I had to put up with at times during the 2001 season, I don't think they're too bad!

The Buttonmania thing took me completely by surprise. What was even more surprising than seeing my own image reflected back at me on a front page was seeing Kim's in some magazine she'd supposedly granted an interview to. That was my first experience of how you can say something and then someone builds it up into something that has a completely different effect. Kim wasn't flattered by the photos they used, and she was pretty upset by the whole thing. I realized very quickly that this was what my life had come to. It was the flipside of the coin, the other side of being a lauded Formula One driver. It goes with the territory.

Instant fame wasn't the only thing I had to cope with. With it came the pressure of expectation. First there was the pressure from the media. It's a subtle process. You suddenly become the new focus of everyone's attention (the papers are always hungry for new sensations). Then, because they have built you up, perhaps into something you are not or can never be, they wait for you to live up to their expectations of you. If you disappoint them, you'd better watch out. I think that's a peculiarly British trait. It's been said many times before, but we seem to like to build people up to be heroes, then cut them down if we think they're getting above themselves.

Then there's the pressure that comes from your fans. I found it difficult at first, because although I've always been into Formula One I've never been into collecting autographs. When I first started I had trouble understanding why people wanted my signature on a piece of paper. Why on earth would they want that? I soon came to realize that any driver, any sportsman, has quite a responsibility to these people. Whether you appreciate it or not, when you have a job like mine you can find yourself the bearer of a lot of people's dreams. For the driver it can be very flattering when people turn out especially to support you, and when they join your fan club. But for them the situation is completely different. I'm not trying to say that we brighten up their dreary lives, or anything patronizing like that, but we can become the focus of their dreams, and that's a heavy burden to carry. Just ask Michael Schumacher.

In many ways you have to carry this responsibility with a lot of care, and that can be very difficult. You may have been working all day, testing, practising, racing or whatever, and you're drained, physically and mentally. It's worse still when you're disappointed after a bad day. You probably don't want to talk to anyone, especially if the car isn't working properly. Maybe you're in a hurry because there's something vital you've just remembered to tell your engineers. But then you have to bear in mind that a lot of these people have been there all day, waiting patiently with their autograph books or with car models they want signed. For some, any driver will do; others will have been waiting specifically for you. And you can bet they've probably paid a fortune just to be there. The way you treat them initially will probably influence their opinion of you for ever. You have to be as kind to them as you can, although obviously you can't spend all day talking to them or signing autographs because you're there to work, and that work goes on long after you've stepped out of the car. You've got the debrief with your engineers, which can go on for hours, maybe a media interview, whatever. But you must give the fans some time.

I find it's best to laugh and joke with them; if they don't all get an autograph by the time you have to leave, at least you've talked to them. In September 2001, for example, I was testing the Benetton-Renault at Silverstone and the place was packed with the biggest crowd I think I'd ever seen at a test. There were just thousands of people milling around the paddock. What happens is that you sign a few autographs, then think you can walk through to the garage and get back to work, but then another thirty people sense activity and rush over to join the throng. Something must be happening, and in a moment they're all around you. It's really difficult. It's not my style to be rude. I wasn't brought up that way. So in situations like that I sign for as many as I can, but you have to keep moving, taking care not to push anyone over. It can get quite claustrophobic at times. I just talk to them, smile and laugh as much as I can.

It was good when I was driving in Formula Three because they do autograph sessions up front there so people don't go away disappointed. It's the same for the touring cars. There's a time set aside for it all. Spectators can buy pit-lane transfers and do the autograph-hunting routine at a specific time, going from garage to garage, the drivers just sitting outside and signing away. It works really well. Few other formulae do that; all the Formula One teams and drivers do something similar, of course, but it doesn't have any 'official' status. It's good training, because it's always good to speak with people and you get to understand the fans. You should see it as quite flattering, so long as they also show an understanding of your situation.

There was a television programme I saw not so long ago about the late actress Yootha Joyce. Somebody was telling a story about how a fan approached her once while she was eating in a restaurant and began to ask for an autograph by saying, 'I'm sorry to interrupt you . . . ' At which point Joyce replied, 'Then why are you?' I couldn't do that. I'm not saying I'd like to be interrupted every time I go out for a quiet dinner with my girlfriend, but it's a give-and-take situation. If people do fail to appreciate a situation and do interrupt, you can just keep it brief. I hope I'm courteous enough to satisfy whatever anyone wants without being standoffish or rude, just as I hope that people will respect my privacy. If you can handle these things with a bit of thought and consideration, there's no reason why everyone can't get what they want.

Sudden 'stardom' is a funny thing, but actually you get to grips with it very quickly. You have to. Especially when you turn up in Australia for your first race and there are people videoing you and wanting to interview you. First of all you like it, because it's flattering. Then you think, 'Jeez. This is hard work!'

I suppose it was inevitable that there would be some sort of backlash to all the hype that surrounded my entry into Formula One. The whole thing was shoved so hard in various faces that I suppose I don't blame some people for disliking the overkill and reacting accordingly. It's human nature. There were certainly plenty of people willing to say that I wasn't serious about my racing, that I was obsessed with all my 'toys'. Well, yeah, I love them! The toys, that is. I think everyone would love to have a 72ft boat, everyone would love to have nice cars or a nice house, which I do. It's the same for everyone in this world, I think. But I've got them and others haven't, and I think that is the problem for some people. When you were twenty, wouldn't you have loved to have a Ferrari 360 Modena? I didn't go out of my way to flaunt mine, but of course I thought it was a mega bit of kit! I happened to be in the fortunate position of being able to buy one, so I did. Where's the problem?

But all these so-called 'toys' also provided people with an excuse for having a pop when things weren't going so well for me with Benetton in 2001. Everything was working out OK the previous year with BMW Williams: why, then, were things suddenly going pear-shaped? Ah, it must be the boat, it must be the house, it must be the cars, it must be his girlfriend, or whatever. I suppose because the results weren't there to back it all up there was a temptation to suggest that my lifestyle was to blame for the poor performance of the cars. But by that logic you would have had to criticize other drivers' lifestyles too, and I don't remember too many journalists' words being wasted on that one. The truth of it is that the boat and other things kept me more focused so I didn't spend much time partying like other drivers, or like I had done the previous year with Williams.

This sort of thing can have a jading effect, but I've managed to avoid that. People like to say things and others have to write about something and you just have to ignore it all. They've got to earn their money, and if they have to do that sort of thing to earn it, fair enough. Benetton boss Flavio Briatore completely understood the situation. He's got a boat too, and he knows that doesn't change the way in which you go about your job. When you're at the circuit you go 100 per cent at what you love doing. The thing I love doing best is racing cars and competing against the best drivers in the world. Owning a boat does not change anything! After a race weekend I sometimes go back to my boat, but it doesn't make me want to leave the circuit any earlier, it doesn't make me think about it when I'm in the pits or on the grid.

The other big pressure I've had to cope with since hitting the headlines is my old kart team boss Paul Lemmens's comment in response to Harald Huysman's question about the three best karters he had ever seen. His response had been, 'Not three, two. Ayrton Senna and Jenson Button.' Obviously that sort of comment is enormously flattering, but it's a double-edged sword. People don't really like that sort of comparison, even though for the media it's manna from heaven. Personally, I don't see anybody being the next

Senna because we're all completely different people and Ayrton was unique. I won't be the next Senna, nobody will.

Besides, I'm much more focused on being the first Jenson Button, and hopefully I will be in the same category as the Brazilian. That's all I've ever wanted.

EIGHT

INTO THE BIG TIME

There were several crazy aspects to my first race in the Big Time. The most ludicrous was that I was in Melbourne at all, at twenty the youngest driver on the grid and one of the youngest ever to sit in a Formula One car, with 800bhp or more at my disposal. I wasn't even old enough to legally hire a road car.

The long-distance travelling was something new, too. Sure, I'd been out to Japan, Korea and America before, but Australia is one hell of a long way away. On one leg on the flight out this guy came down and sat next to us. It was the jockey Frankie Dettori. Dad and I were getting a little bit sleepy, but Frankie soon put a stop to that. 'Hey, I know you!' he said. 'You're the one I failed that question about on *Question of Sport*!' The programme had shown my photo as part of round one and Frankie hadn't known who I was. Then he started talking about horse racing, explaining things such as what he did to put the brakes on a horse. He sat there, in first class, adopting the riding posture in his seat as if he had reins in his hands. Very funny.

Due to all the publicity I'd had before I'd even done my first race, people were beginning to recognize me on the plane and in the airports. It was all a bit overwhelming, though I'm not one to shy away from publicity. But the sheer intensity of it all did take me by surprise. I think the fact that my story so far read like some sort of Hollywood script just captured everyone's imagination. You have to take these things in your stride, but it helps if you don't find it a chore. I know some drivers who hate it, but it's all part of the deal. There's no two ways about it – I love it. And I think that's a reason why I haven't changed as a person since my karting days. Sure, I've grown up. That's inevitable. And I've learned a huge amount and am still learning, but I don't think I've changed fundamentally as a bloke.

I've never been much of a one for discussing things in great detail. That's not because I don't like to think things through, it's just never been my style to rake through everything endlessly, although I'm quite introspective. I like to keep some things to myself, but I don't dwell on them. Dad learned early on not to push me in this direction, and we have developed an understanding. There was one hell of a lot of pressure on me going into that first race on 12 March, but I suppose the thing I was telling him most was, 'Don't worry, Dad. I can handle it.' And inside I knew full well that I could. Some people were expecting me to be cowed by it all, but I was actually loving every moment.

Dad and I went out a week early so that I could get fully acclimatized. When we arrived at Melbourne's airport we were met by a limo driver who'd been hired to pick us up. He was tall and wore a uniform and peaked cap. He kept calling me sir. It was gone three o'clock in the morning and we were quite close to our hotel, but after he'd asked what I did for a living, he turned round and said, 'Would sir like to go round the circuit?' I said, 'Yeah, go for it!'

So he did two laps for us, full beam on, animals scuttling across the road. Dad and I just died laughing in the back. This guy didn't know the circuit at all really, but when he was driving on the straights he was saying things like, 'You need full power here,' then getting to a corner and saying, 'You have to brake here.' Of course he meant well, but it was just so funny. I guess he thought I was so young that I needed all the help I could get. It was a good start, even though I fell asleep in the back halfway round his second lap!

The following day I drove round in a BMW and it was an odd feeling because Albert Park hadn't yet become a pukka race track. Here was everything I'd seen before on television, and suddenly there I was, on the actual track which wasn't quite a bona fide track yet. People were all over the place, building things. It was an incredible feeling, even if it still didn't quite seem real.

People in the media tend to make a lot of fuss about drivers learning new circuits, and of course for me a lot of the tracks on the Formula One calendar were going to be new. When I started I knew only Silverstone, Hockenheim and Spa from a racing perspective, though I'd also tested at Barcelona and Magny-Cours. But any decent driver will learn a track within a couple of laps. Some like to walk round them; others play computer games; others drive round in hire cars. All of that helps to remind you that the next corner is a sharp left-hander, or whatever, but that's as far as it goes. The best way to learn how to drive a Formula One car around a track is to drive a Formula One car around it. A hire car bears no resemblance to the way the track will flow for you in the real thing. There's no comparison whatsoever.

I quite liked the fact that to begin with Dad and I could just walk across from the hotel without being recognized. We did silly things together, like meeting Mandy the koala at the zoo (I reckon she was stoned on eucalyptus). There were also sponsor functions and photoshoots to attend. As the race drew closer the numbers of guards and fans grew. More recognition, more media attention. It was a real buzz. I could feel everything beginning to build up.

Right from the moment I started with BMW Williams, people helped me to settle in. One nice touch was when I arrived at the track one day to find that my side of the garage and my pit board now bore the St George cross of England at Frank's behest. He also asked me to have one on the belt of my race suit. I thought that was cool, although I hoped it wouldn't offend other people in Britain, the Scots, the Welsh and the Northern Irish, because we're all part of the same country and I value them as fellow countrymen just as much as I do Englishmen. But David Coulthard wears the saltire and Scottish flag, and he seems to keep everyone happy!

After the testing I'd done in the car, and my competitive speeds in comparison with Ralf Schumacher's, I went to Melbourne secretly believing that I could qualify in the top ten. Given the right car and situation, I thought that was feasible. But events were to militate against that in a big way.

To begin with things went quite well: I was firmly in the respectable half of the timesheets. On the first day I drove forty incident-free laps round a slippery Albert Park, usually in five-lap stints. I started off cautiously, though I was the second guy out when practice began because I wanted as much track time as I could get. Only Ricardo Zonta went out ahead of me. During the first half an hour my best time was good enough to be second fastest, which was fun. I was fiddling with the set-up, but just after I'd got within a few tenths of Ralf in the afternoon a bird hit my car and its carcass was catapulted into the cockpit. It was a scary moment, but it had already happened to me that year during testing at Kyalami, so I was getting used to it. But I don't think feathers suit me! I finished the day in eighteenth place, having mainly focused on race set-up. I was pleased to be close to Ralf. He'd done a 1m 34.158s lap for sixteenth place, and I did 1m 34.547s.

Those sessions were really all about learning the circuit and working with the team on the set-up, and that went well. There were few surprises, though I was amazed by how slow some of the corners were in Melbourne. I hoped they would get faster as the weekend wore on and more rubber got laid down. It was still difficult for a lot of people to pass judgements and speak about me being in Formula One because they didn't know me as a person or, really, as a driver. But if you're ready for Formula One, then you're ready. It doesn't matter what age you are, within reason. There's a lot of pressure on you, especially outside the car, but the driving is the most important part. It's definitely not the easiest part, of course, but that day I think I did OK.

I know what Jenson was going through because three years earlier I was the kart graduate moving into Formula One after only eighteen months in Formula Three cars. Jenson and I never raced together, but very often we were at the same meetings, so I had known him a long time. I couldn't give him advice about Formula One; he knew what he had to do. Just get as much mileage as possible. I knew that as soon as he felt comfortable he would be quick because he is talented. He is OK, so he would quickly understand what to do.

Jarno Trulli, Formula One driver, Jordan

I gave the sceptics what they'd been waiting for on the Saturday morning. I lost control of the car in the fast kink near Turn Seven, Marina. I smacked pretty hard into the wall, which ended my session and immediately compromised my chances of qualifying well. I was really, really hacked off with myself for doing that. I don't shunt much, never have, yet here I was at the most important race of my career, damaging the car. I was pushing too hard, too early. I just hooked a wheel on the kerb and round the car came. I didn't think it was going to be a drama because I wasn't going very fast, only about 160mph. Some people said it was probably the best thing I could have done because it gave the media what they were expecting and got it out of the way, but when you're in the cockpit you never see things that way. All I could see was that I had let myself and the team down, spilled ink over my homework. And I'd given myself a mountain to climb for qualifying. As it transpired, it was one of the few times I damaged a car all year, but at the time I was really angry with myself.

It wasn't a massive accident. I just got a bit out of shape, got on to the grass, and that was it. So by the time I had hitched a ride back to the pits things didn't seem quite so bad, and everyone was quite good about it. I suppose some of them felt that it had to happen, but really I hadn't gone to Australia expecting to do that. I'd hoped to do what I had been doing up until the point I went off: running in the top ten during free practice.

The legacy of the crash was missing the rest of the session, which is valuable track time when you're working to set the car up not only for qualifying but also for the race. On a Friday you get into your programme of setting the car up with a reasonable amount of fuel aboard, working a lot on race set-up. Some people like to do a quick lap towards the end of the day with low fuel, but Williams rarely indulged in that. You also assess the two tyre options and try to figure out which is better suited to the track. We have to make our choice prior to qualifying, when you can only use one type of tyre and then have to use that in the race as well. During free practice on Saturday morning you do some more work on that, then set the car up for qualifying. So I'd blown all that and had to go into the all-important afternoon session much less well prepared than I'd intended.

Under the circumstances, the team did a fabulous job to get the car ready again for qualifying, and to be honest the morning's accident didn't create any psychological problems for me. I was ready to get the job done. Unfortunately, the car developed a fuel pick-up problem during my first two runs. When I went for full throttle sometimes the engine just cut out. I had to come back to the pits again and take over the spare, which was set up for Ralf. I struggled with it and got caught in one of the FIA's random weight checks, as luck would have it. When I eventually got out again there were yellow flags everywhere, and finally a red after David Coulthard crashed. So in the end I qualified in twenty-first place for my first Grand Prix. I was on the back row alongside Gastón Mazzacane in his Minardi. Ralf was eleventh with a lap time of 1m 32.220s compared to my 1m 33.828s.

I felt absolutely gutted. I felt I had let myself and everyone else down. Some people were kind enough to say that it wasn't my fault, that these things happen, but I felt it was. I'd so wanted to do well, to show what I could do, and there I was, on the back row of the grid for my Formula One début. I'd kept my aspirations to myself, of course, but I really had believed that a top-ten grid place was possible. And it should have been.

I think the way the team handled things over those two days showed the strength of the relationship we had forged even by that early stage – although every time I talked to Frank or Patrick for the first couple of months I have to admit that I felt like a schoolboy in front of his headmaster. I was never quite sure what to say. They'd ask, 'How's it going, Jenson?' and I'd say, 'Okay, I'm getting to grips with it!' And then I'd run out of things to say. I just wouldn't know what to say next. It was very difficult for me, but Frank was always smiling and saying, 'Just get on with your job, just work with the team.' He'd also ask, 'How's your fitness, Jenson?' Every conversation we had, that would crop up. 'How's your fitness, Jenson? How's it going?' But that was a good thing. He was always caring and worrying about the fitness side of things.

Patrick was the same, though initially I found him less easy to talk to. I knew that against expectations he and Alex Zanardi hadn't hit things off, even though Alex had a reputation as a driver who really understood the technical side of the cars, which should have appealed to Patrick. I didn't know anything like as much as Alex about the technology, so I wasn't really sure how to proceed.

I think one factor on my side was my youth. They treated me like I was a kid, which was a good thing in one way: I was lacking experience, so if I made a little mistake or whatever they were quite easy on me. When I started doing well, it was more of a shock to them than anything else. If I had a good session and qualified well, then had a bad one, they weren't too worried about it. They knew that I just had to get more experience. That was a good thing for me, it really was.

I was the youngest Briton ever to step on to a Grand Prix grid, taking over that 'honour' from Stirling Moss. But I wasn't the youngest guy ever: Mike Thackwell, Ricardo Rodriguez, Estebán Tuero and Chris Amon all started even younger than I did. The start is always the highest pressure moment of a race weekend, and there had already been massive speculation about how I would perform. Stirling Moss said he didn't think I was too young, but that it was amazing that I could be young and in the position I was in. He thought if I could rise to the occasion I could become a big name. But Jackie Stewart was concerned for me, and questioned whether I was really ready for Formula One. He had always believed that I had graduated too soon. 'If Einstein hadn't gone through the full school curriculum,' he observed, 'he would have had something missing from his years of learning. You have to learn about life as well as racing, and Formula One is not the place to learn about life.' Fellow racer Mika Salo, who had qualified tenth for Sauber Petronas, had also been quoted saying some critical things about the danger I presented as an inexperienced rookie (though later he had the grace to apologize). Former team owner Ken Tyrrell said that he expected I would have my eyes opened when we all began that adrenalin rush down to the first corner, but said it in a nice way.

I always thought that stuff about the way the first corner would sort him out was a load of bollocks. If the people who said that saw the start of a Super A kart race, with thirty of the world's best karters all vying for position, they'd appreciate that Jens will feel a lot safer sitting in a carbon-fibre monocoque chassis. Every circuit has a first corner, so what's the big deal?

John Button

The race went much better for me than qualifying, especially as I'd given myself a boost in the morning warm-up with the third fastest time. Actually, I thought my first Grand Prix start was a real gas! When the red lights finally went out and my Formula One career really began, I just thought, 'Jesus!' It was a lot more mad than I thought it was going to be. People move around a lot on the circuit in lower formulae, but they can do it stupidly. In Formula One, everyone is really aware. They do it properly. Everyone is moving intelligently, trying to get into the little spaces. It's really, really strange.

I was pretty opportunistic on that first lap because I knew that the best time to make places was at the start, before people settled into their rhythm. And I was a bit lucky, too, with people dropping out. I seemed to be in the right places at the right times. At the same time, I was trying to take it easy. In the first corner Pedro Diniz's Sauber collided with Nick Heidfeld's Prost, and I just missed them. I thought for one terrible moment my race was going to end there and then. Then I passed Marc Gené's Minardi going into the second corner, then Johnny Herbert as his Jaguar lost its clutch. I made up five places. Then I got on the dirt on the third lap and Alex Wurz passed me, and there was a shunt involving Eddie Irvine and Pedro de la Rosa. After that I managed to settle into a rhythm, and I was really enjoying myself. The race was over fifty-eight laps, and by half distance I was running eleventh, chasing Wurz's Benetton. Ralf was eighth and our lap times were comparable. After all the tension of the shootout, after all the publicity surrounding my selection, and after all the pressure building up to the race, I felt relaxed and happy. I was doing what I really wanted to do, and things were going well.

I moved up a place when Salo stopped for fuel, two more when Rubens Barrichello and Ricardo Zonta did likewise, and was actually as high as fourth on lap thirty-six as I was one of the last to come in for fuel. I rejoined in seventh place, and maintained that ahead of Zonta and Salo. When Heinz-Harald Frentzen retired on lap forty I moved into sixth place. For the next seven laps I had a World Championship point almost in my pocket, first time out, and was catching Giancarlo Fisichella and Jacques Villeneuve ahead. I was just thinking, 'Villeneuve's been world champion,' when something went wrong in the engine. Suddenly, it was all over.

Of course it was a massive disappointment in some ways, though not in others. And it was good to see Ralf finishing third. I'm not a great one for the historical aspects of the sport, but I knew that many of the top drivers had scored points on their début and I wanted to do the same thing. All the time I was running sixth I was just praying that everything would hold together. There was also that thing about being the youngest guy to score a point. I didn't pay an awful lot of attention to it, but the media was getting quite stoked up about it and I have to admit it did cross my mind that it would be quite a cool thing to do. But there you are. Formula One is like any other form of motorsport: it has highs and it has lows. You have to learn to accept and move on. I felt that I'd proved something, and that was what mattered most to me. I felt that I'd shown I did deserve my Formula One berth, despite what my critics had said. I felt that I had shown I belonged in the fraternity.

Looking back on my début, I was quite pleased with the way I'd handled things – the Saturday shunt apart – and that none of the side issues or hype had intruded on the way I did my job. I'd even survived my first turn 'in the bucket', as the drivers say, at one of the official 'Friday Five' media sessions, for which the FIA chooses five drivers who are then obliged to subject themselves to a grilling. It can be a bit nerve-racking, because the drivers on the selected panel have questions fired at them by the FIA's official race commentator Bob Constanduros, who always asks pertinent things, and then it's opened up to questions from the floor. Generally my first taste of this went quite well, and I was told afterwards that I scored Brownie points for the way I handled some daft questions from local journalists about hairstyles and whether or not I liked warm beer!

I think the toughest part of the race weekend, and the biggest lesson I learned, was coping with the disappointment of a feeble qualifying performance. Immediately afterwards the media wanted

to grill me on the reasons for my failure to live up to their expectations, and the last thing I wanted to do right then was talk to
anyone outside the team. I mean, I really didn't want to do that.
That was when I came to appreciate the true nature of that side of
the job.

For them, I was one of the big stories. The British national newspapers had built me up and plastered me all over their front pages
when I got the drive. Everything was hunky-dory then, but now I
had failed to deliver and they all wanted to know why, right there
and then. I began to realize that publicity can be a double-edged
sword. James Hunt, Nigel Mansell and Damon Hill had all discovered the same thing, but it's something you have to learn for
yourself, in your own specific situations. I'm told that as a British
driver you are often one of the reasons why national papers
continue to cover Formula One. I'm sure it's the same for David
Coulthard and Eddie Irvine, and other national standard bearers.
England expects, and all that. Inevitably you are a focus of the
papers' stories.

I wanted and needed a bit of time to recover from my disappointment, but I wasn't going to get it. I was hurting, I wanted to
talk with my engineers, get my head straight, try to figure out what
had gone wrong. But one journalist made it crystal clear that it
would be worse for me if I didn't come out and face the inquisition.
That was difficult, having to steel myself to grin and bear it when
it was the last thing I wanted to do. But that goes with the badge,
I guess.

To be fair, the media guys have a job to do too, and most of them
are pretty responsible and I get on well with them. But their job
really begins right after we've done the most visible part of ours.
They have deadlines that clash with our debriefs, so the two
things will not always be mutually compatible. And I got a pretty

understanding press from it all in the end, so no complaints there. But it was an eye-opener. I began to realize that there is a quid pro quo in the relationship. I would also come to appreciate that a significant degree of motorsport journalism these days is more about human politics and lifestyle than it is about what actually happens on the race track. It was never like that in the relatively non-political world of Formula Three, let alone karting.

I outqualified Ralf for my second Grand Prix, a fortnight later in Brazil. I might not have got my top-ten grid position in Melbourne, but I was absolutely delighted to get it second time out.

Interlagos is in São Paulo, and I'd never seen the track before. It's a difficult, technical circuit with a lot of very high-speed corners and some tricky infield turns that make set-up critical. Things were difficult in practice, when two separate engine faults lost me a lot of valuable track time. On the Friday I did twenty-three laps in the morning, but after only four in the afternoon the engine developed a problem. That was a bit frustrating, because though my best lap left me twentieth it had been pretty competitive for the tyre and track conditions when I actually set it. My car needed another engine change between free practice on Saturday morning and qualifying. Then, just before qualifying, the skies began to cloud over. As the session progressed I just got my head down and worked away with my engineer Tim Preston. The car felt really good.

I was very lucky to have Tim as my engineer in my first season. He knows a lot about Formula One and was able to point me in the right direction when I needed it. We got on really well, and were always having a laugh together. He was always finding something about me that he could take the piss out of, and I was just the same with him. He was great, really good fun. He grew his beard when I had mine. He's a character, quite a groovy bloke. We used to call him The Poet, with all his hair.

I was in the pits with Frank's team that day, and I had a set of headphones so I could listen in. Jenson was very impressive. He knew exactly what he wanted from the car, and it was him that was telling Tim Preston what he wanted. 'A bit stiffer at the front, drop the wing a bit at the back,' that sort of thing. He was the one calling the changes to the car. He was cool and calm, and to do that well first time out on a driver's track spoke volumes for him.

Russell Spence, former F3000 and F3 racer

There was a very strange atmosphere in the garage after qualifying, because obviously Ralf, who finished eleventh just as he'd done in Melbourne, was very annoyed. I don't think the session went very well for him. He wasn't happy at all. We'd got my car out at the right time. I was just sitting in the garage in my car afterwards, I'd done my lap time of 1m 15.490s, and I was actually sixth fastest for a while. I was looking at my timing screen, thinking, 'Oh my God, I hope it rains now!' It got very close to doing just that, although unfortunately it didn't. Then Ralf went out and lapped a tenth or two slower, and I thought, 'He's going to have me on the next run.' But he didn't. I just sat in the car waiting for people to go quicker, and only three did, so I was ninth on the grid. It was just the most amazing feeling, seeing the mechanics smiling at me. A great moment.

We used to follow Ralf's set-up at the start, in testing and in Melbourne, but not in Brazil. We have different styles, so we had to work quite a bit to get things right. It was good to outqualify him at Interlagos, but it was good for him too because I was then in a position to help him out with his set-up. He was the number one driver and we were helping each other out. We had a good relationship. I know I didn't have as much experience in racing as many of the drivers on the grid, but in qualifying I'd shown I could hack it. As I got out of the car I walked past Patrick, and he said, 'Well done, Jenson!' That was all he said, really. But it spoke volumes.

I made a crap start in the race, which really annoyed me. It was quite possibly the worst start I've ever made. I got too much wheel-spin on and bogged the thing down, so I was down to thirteenth place by the end of the first lap. Then Jean Alesi overtook me on the second. I settled down to a waiting game. I managed to pass Villeneuve on the ninth lap and began to chase down Ralf, who had also been slow off the line. Gradually we both moved back up through the pack, and when I stopped for fuel after forty-four of the seventy-one laps Ralf was fifth and I was sixth. I had dropped behind Frentzen and Verstappen by the time I rejoined, but I hunted the latter down and managed to overtake him on the fifty-sixth lap. By the finish it looked as though Ralf and I had finished sixth and seventh respectively. I was pleased to finish the race and delighted that my best lap was slightly faster than Ralf's, but very disappointed to have missed out on a championship point.

But Fate had a card left to play. I was at the airport preparing to fly home when news came through that David Coulthard had been disqualified from second place for a front-wing illegality. I was sixth after all. It was a funny way to score my first World Championship point, but you take them any way they come.

It wasn't long before somebody worked out the maths as we celebrated. I had indeed just become, at twenty years and sixty-seven days old, the youngest driver in the history of Formula One to score a World Championship point. At the end of the season a paragraph in the *Autocourse* annual finished: '. . . there is a bold and audacious streak in the young Englishman, tempered by remarkable maturity and self-control. In many ways, Button's was the most telling individual performance of the race.' Which I thought was a nice compliment.

Things came a bit unglued when we arrived in Imola for the San Marino Grand Prix on 9 April. The FW22 was obviously pretty good round there, but I really didn't do it justice in practice or qualifying. Imola is quite a tight little circuit, with some key chicanes such as the Variante Bassa at the end of the lap and the Variante Alfa at the highest point, and there are new kinks at Tamburello and Villeneuve and a section at Acque Minerale all of which require you to use the kerbs. I freely confess that I just didn't get to grips with that aspect of things on the Friday or the Saturday. I like to be as smooth as possible and not to throw the car about or bully it, so I was tending to stay clear of the kerbs. It took me a while to figure it all out. Ralf qualified fifth on 1m 25.871s, while I struggled to 1m 27.135s and a lowly eighteenth place. I wasn't very impressed with myself.

I had a long think on Saturday night and talked things through with people in the team, and Sunday morning's race warm-up was a lot better as a result. I forgot about delicacy and just hammered the car over the kerbs; the result was eleventh fastest time. It was a step in the right direction. The race, though, was a bust. I'd got up to sixteenth after five laps when the engine just let go.

The next race was the British Grand Prix, which had been moved to April because of some political wrangling that resulted in the Austrian race taking the mid-July slot. The 2000 meet became infamous as the race of the muddy car parks, thousands of spectators having to endure horrible weather and terrible conditions as they flocked into Silverstone. But for me it was wonderful.

I'd really been looking forward to driving in front of my home crowd on a circuit on which I had previous experience. Right from the start I was able to push hard: I was eleventh fastest in Friday practice but twenty-first after a few problems on Saturday morning. I had a mega spin in the wet and lost a load of running time after Eddie Irvine spun his Jaguar at the same place and did a lot of damage to my car. It felt like Melbourne all over again, but this time I managed to get it all together and keep it there to qualify sixth. I was pretty pleased with that. Rubens Barrichello and Heinz-Harald Frentzen shared the front row, for Ferrari and Jordan respectively, and the McLarens of Mika Hakkinen and David Coulthard were on the second. On row three I sat alongside Michael Schumacher. I could hardly believe it! It was a fantastic feeling, and I had to keep reminding myself that the last time I'd raced at the circuit, late the previous season, I'd still been in Formula Three.

At the start Michael swept to the outside, got two wheels on the grass and was boxed in by the time we all got to Copse corner, so as Barrichello led Frentzen, Coulthard and Hakkinen I was able to slice inside Michael to snatch fifth place. It felt mega knowing that I had the World Championship leader behind me. I lost some time and a place to Ralf during my first pit stop on the twenty-fifth lap, then picked up behind him as we ran in fourth and fifth places. I had a brief spell in third place during the second round of stops, but Ralf and I resumed our positions as soon as the pit-stop dust settled.

Towards the end of the race the engine began to sound really rough. An exhaust had cracked, and I spent the rest of my afternoon praying that the thing would last. It was a massive relief to see the chequered flag in fifth place, and to score another pair of points.

When we'd gone to Australia Jenson still had very limited mileage because we'd had a lot of unreliability problems. We had not managed more than a hundred kilometres in one sustained burst with the car. So Jenson went there with that handicap, plus the onus of a lot of media attention. You could see that although he was coping with it, he wasn't the same relaxed person he'd been at the tests. He had trouble with the car on Friday. Then when he went off on the Saturday morning it was a pretty big one. It wasn't a light one, he didn't just tap a wing. His demeanour was different then; he was a man under pressure. But he did a good job in the race. It was worthy of a point but for the engine letting go.

By Brazil he'd got his act together. It was a difficult situation because it was damp, spitting with rain. And he did a good job. Where Ralf was very strong was that he was going into his fourth year in Formula One and had a huge database of knowledge. He'd turn up at a given circuit and know, for example, that it was dirty off line. He'd know the peculiarities of the circuit and what he had to do with his car. Whereas Jenson didn't have that database of information so he was going there and starting at a disadvantage. That's what was so impressive about outqualifying Ralf at Interlagos. It was a fantastic job, and in difficult circumstances.

He struggled at Imola because he didn't really have that much experience of the need to ride the kerbs. He didn't understand that perhaps until race-day morning. Then he was OK. And I thought he was sensational at Silverstone.

Jim Wright, Head of Marketing, Williams F1 team

I'd had my share of mechanical problems, usually in practice, in each of the four races I'd driven in, but in that time I had out-qualified my team-mate twice and had finished in the points twice, scoring three. And I had enjoyed a spell ahead of Michael Schumacher. I didn't think that was bad for a twenty-year-old.

But what I really wanted to know was whether these levels of performance were good enough to enable me to hang on to my seat at BMW Williams for 2001.

NINE

OVER BEFORE IT'S STARTED?

I suffered a bit of a performance dip after Silverstone, and it was a prelude to massive uncertainty about my future, which blew up around the time of the Monaco Grand Prix at the beginning of June. My form set people wondering whether my Formula One career was over almost before it had begun.

My fifth race in the Big League was the Spanish Grand Prix on 7 May at the Circuit de Catalunya in Barcelona, which was by now another track with which I was wholly familiar. Ralf was in strong form there, and qualified fifth. I lined up eleventh after the wind seemed to blow my car all over the place, but conditions improved on race day and I was fifth in the morning warm-up. Both of us went for a two-stop strategy in the race. Ralf quickly got up to third place after passing Barrichello and Coulthard, while I got the jump on Irvine and overtook his Jaguar. As the first round of pit stops approached, we were running in third and ninth places respectively. After my stop I had worked my way up to sixth place with four laps left to run and was looking forward to scoring some more points when the engine let go without any warning. Ralf had better luck with his car and went on to finish fourth after a brush with his brother cost him a place on the podium. All I had to take home was the fourth fastest race lap. Nevertheless, BMW Williams maintained third place in the Constructors Championship.

At the Nürburgring two weeks later for the Grand Prix of Europe, I should have scored some more points but was frustrated by a freak occurrence in the race. Ralf and I qualified fifth and eleventh again, just three tenths of a second apart, on another circuit that was new to me; I'd lost a bit of ground on him and the others after an off in practice. Towards the end of the race I was fighting hard with Johnny Herbert for a point. It was a wet race, my first in Formula One, and conditions were pretty horrible, especially as I was running right behind the Jaguar and couldn't see anything when we were travelling at speed down the straights. In the slower corners it wasn't so bad because the spray decreased, but if you imagine what it's like in torrential rain on the motorway, then take away your windscreen, your wipers and luxuries such as a nice heater, then double or triple the speed, you can begin to get an idea what it was like. The scariest bit was when it started to rain and we were still out on dry tyres. I had some massive moments, although I was going pretty quickly in relation to a lot of the others at that stage. If we'd got our pit strategy better and come in sooner for wets, I think I'd have scored some decent points.

I knew I was quicker than Johnny, but passing him was always going to be tricky. On one lap I got right up behind him at one of the slow corners, but he braked quite hard and I slid into the back of his car. It was only a gentle nudge, though, and we both stayed on the track. Everything seemed fine, but the contact, unknown to me, had punctured a hole in the leading edge of my car's nose. That let sufficient rain in to affect the electrical system, and all of a sudden, with just five laps to run and with me in seventh place, the car quit on me. I was beginning to get a bit bored with stopping so close to the finish of a Grand Prix.

Then came Monaco. This is the jewel in the Formula One crown. There is no other race like it in the world. The nearest thing I had experienced before I went there was the Macau Grand Prix back in my Formula Three days. Even before the meeting got under way rumours about my future began to flood the paddock. Juan Pablo Montoya was going to replace me at BMW Williams in 2001; I was virtually out of work.

In the past, Frank and Patrick have taken an awful lot of flak from the media. In 1992 they fell out with Nigel Mansell just as he was on the verge of winning his World Championship, and they failed to agree terms for 1993. Nigel went off to America, where he won the IndyCar Championship at the first attempt. At one stage the *Sun* newspaper launched a campaign against Williams, and even had protesters and Page Three girls picketing the old factory in Didcot. Then, in 1996 almost exactly the same thing happened with Damon Hill. He was charging along to his world title, and the team had already decided to replace him with Heinz-Harald Frentzen for 1997. There was a massive outcry when Andrew Benson broke the news to the world – and to Damon, it seemed – in *Autosport* in the middle of the season. Now the media was warming up in my defence, thinking that I was about to be screwed by the callous team owners.

Actually, what really happened showed the true calibre of Frank and Patrick. The reality is that right from the moment I was taken on with BMW Williams, I knew about the situation with Montoya; I knew there would be a good chance that I would be in the team for only a year. Montoya had been the test driver for Williams during his time in Formula 3000, and he had a handshake deal with

Frank. And contrary to what people might like to think, Frank is very honourable like that. Moreover, he told me all this. He said that it wasn't 100 per cent certain that Montoya would be coming, but I knew right from the start there was the possibility that my tenancy of the seat alongside Ralf would probably be shortlived. Ralf himself had another year to run on his contract, which would take him through to 2001, so there was a clear chance of a three into two situation. Frankly, I wasn't sure there was ever anything I could have done about it.

In any case, I didn't let myself dwell on the situation because I just wanted to get on and prove what I could do. What didn't help as far as media gossip was concerned was that a lot of people around this time put two and two – my drop-off in form, the unreliability of my car – together and ended up with five. We had problems with the BMW engines around that time. I don't know quite what the true nature of those problems was, but I was certainly blowing up a lot of engines for some reason. BMW had already backed off 50bhp in the interests of reliability, and we didn't seem to compete so well for a while until they solved the problem from Hockenheim on 30 July onwards.

But the problems weren't all down to BMW Williams. I had pretty much set the car up myself for Interlagos and Silverstone, working with Tim Preston, but I tried to go my own way a little too much after that and it didn't work. As I got a bit more experience towards the end of the year that approach would start to work for me again, and I think that's what made the difference in the second half of 2000 when I was back on the pace. But at this point I wasn't getting as much out of the car in qualifying as Ralf was. That played into the hands of those who were starting up the doom-and-gloom 'Jenson out' stories.

I also had some mechanical problems at race meetings, in

practice and qualifying or during the warm-up, which few people knew about but which lost me big chunks of track time. We had a fuel pick-up problem in some qualifying sessions, such as the one in Melbourne. It was that rather than the shunt that had left me twenty-first on the grid. People tended to overlook these issues. They'd just look at wherever I'd qualified on the grid and immediately dismiss it as the result of inexperience.

There was a little bit of a dip for Jenson after Silverstone. And we had a bit of a dip in form ourselves, when BMW had to detune the engines by 50bhp to keep them alive in races. You needed experience to avoid compromising the set-up of the car and we lost our way a little bit. But when we became strong again, Jenson just grew from that.

Jim Wright, Head of Marketing, Williams F1 team

Of course there was a degree of uncertainty about my future because Frank hadn't completely decided about Montoya, but not only did I know about the situation, I also had a long-term contract with the team in my briefcase, so I knew things were brighter than they might have looked to others. I was confident I would be driving *something* in Formula One in 2001.

The actual driving at Monaco wasn't a problem for me while all this speculation about my future was raging around me, because whenever I was in the car I concentrated totally on my job, which was to drive the car to its limit. So I had no problems in that respect during practice, qualifying or the race. But things did get a bit difficult whenever I had to get out of the car. There were people all over the place asking the same question over and over again; I'd be a liar if I said I didn't find that irritating. Anyone would feel the same if they were constantly being asked about the likelihood of being dropped when they were trying to work. What goes on off the circuit is a very important part of Formula One, of course, but for me it's not *the* most important part. For me, the most important thing is driving, and I felt fine when I was out on the circuit doing that. David and Harald were focused on the employment situation on my behalf, but I'm a hands-on sort of person and naturally I get involved quite a bit (after all, if I wasn't here there wouldn't be anything up for negotiation). But I certainly don't let myself get involved with all that during race weekends. My priority then is simply to relax and concentrate on the job in hand.

As far as my position was concerned, what the whole situation boiled down to was this: in order to have kept Montoya out of the car for 2001 I would have had to do something spectacular in the first half of the year. And that wasn't exactly on the cards in my first ever season in Formula One. Interlagos and Silverstone were great, sure, but some of the other races weren't. Part of that was down to me, part of it was the car. As for what might have happened had the judgement been made based on the second half of the season, that's academic.

We were told it was up to Jenson, and what he achieved. It was up to him to stop Montoya coming back. That's what we were told. In the end we went through a messy stage with the team, obviously, but none of it affected Jenson's driving, though people said it did. They said that when he knew he was being replaced and was going elsewhere then the rejuvenated Jenson changed at the end of the year. That simply wasn't true. He gave every-thing all the time, but in the latter part of the year when the engine power was put back up and the car was sorted he was able to run really well.

Frank kept saying good things in 2000 about Jenson

that made even me, his father and greatest supporter, embarrassed. He told me once that Jens was 'almost perfect' and that he'd only ever had one driver like that before, though he wouldn't say who. He said to me at one point, 'You know, I think I might have made the biggest mistake of my life in letting Jenson go.' He denied saying that just to make me happy. I thought, 'I know what I'm going to do for Frank. I'm going to protect him. All this talk about what he did with Mansell and what he did with Hill, I'm going to tell the press that we knew for sure at the beginning of the year that Montoya was coming back.' Frank had given Jenson a chance, had treated him very, very well and didn't put any pressure on him, so we will protect him on this one. A few weeks later, some moron in the media wrote that Jenson had the cheek to say that he did not know in the beginning that Montoya was coming back. But I didn't want the press ripping Frank to pieces after he'd given Jens a chance. Others wanted to give Frank a hard time, but that was the way to do it. It was done nicely. And that all helps.

John Button

What happened was that Frank said, 'I also have an option on Montoya, so I want to sign Jenson on a long-term deal. I might have to let Jenson go for a couple of years, because I have Montoya to look at as well. I might. Let's see how Jenson goes.' So it was really up to Jenson to be sensational.

And there was another thing to bear in mind. If you look at Kimi [Raikkonen], he had thousands of kilometres of testing before he got into his first race. I think he'd done around six thousand kilometres before Melbourne

in 2001. In Jenson's case there was actually speculation that he wouldn't get his superlicence [the licence issued by the FIA that qualifies someone to drive in Formula One] because he hadn't done enough testing because of the technical problems, and most of what he'd done was in the wet. Jenson was sensational in the second half of 2000, after Frank had already decided about Montoya, but initially Jenson really was thrown in at the mega deep end. He was well shy on the mileage.

David Robertson

My first Monaco Grand Prix, then, was an unusual affair. In practice I completed 101 trouble- and incident-free laps, which I was quite pleased about. But less pleasing was my failure to get only one clear run out of my four in qualifying. The car was understeering badly. It lacked good traction and didn't feel great under the brakes either, so that all left me fourteenth on the grid when I was convinced a top-ten place wasn't out of the question. Ralf was ninth.

This was the race that needed three starts. First, Alexander Wurz's Benetton cut out on the grid; it turned out his engine had broken. Then I collided with Pedro de la Rosa's Arrows at the Loews hairpin on the first lap when he cut across me. Pedro Diniz and Nick Heidfeld were caught up as well, and the track was blocked. They red-flagged that restart and gave us time to sprint the two kilometres back to the pits (that's another reason why we have to be fit!). Third time around I started from the pit lane in the spare car, which was set up for Ralf. It didn't feel great right from the start, and I was lying only nineteenth after seventeen laps when the team called me in. The telemetry indicated that I was losing oil, so with another engine failure imminent there was no point carrying on. It was a disappointing end to a disappointing weekend.

> **The team had expected Monaco to be tough for Jenson, but he didn't put a mark on the car. To go there and not put a mark on the car with his limited level of experience, and it was certainly not disgraceful in terms of performance, was bloody impressive. That certainly was not the turning point that made us decide to go with Juan Pablo. Having picked the Colombian up at an early stage and run with him, had we not then gone with him we'd have lost him. He would have gone to another team, and it would have been crazy.**
>
> Jonathan Williams, BMW Williams

The next race took place in Canada on 18 June, at the Circuit Gilles Villeneuve on the Ile Notre Dame just outside Montreal, a fantastic city. It was the eighth event on the calendar, and I was almost halfway through my rookie season. I wanted to get things back on track, and was determined I was going to come away with some more points. Once again, however, fate was going to deny me.

It was at this meet that Frank Williams first gave David Robertson a real hint as to what was going to happen in terms of the driving arrangements at Williams for 2001. David asked Frank outright if we should be talking to other teams, and Frank replied that there would be no harm in doing so. We figured, rightly, that he was just waiting for Montoya's confirmation. Frank was contractually bound to inform us one way or the other by the end of July in any case. The official decision in favour of the Colombian actually came a month sooner than that, so from that moment on David and Harald were truly free to set up another deal for me.

But that was all happening off the track. On it, both Ralf and I struggled all weekend in Montreal to set our cars up, and it's fair to say that we lost our way a little. He started the race twelfth on the grid; I was only half a second slower, but that left me six places lower. The track highlighted the FW22's problem: it preferred medium- to high-speed corners rather than the slow stuff in Montreal. But I was also hampered by a return of the fuel pick-up problem, which again meant that my engine kept cutting at maximum revs.

When race day dawned overcast and the weather looked changeable, however, I thought I stood a pretty good chance, even though it's harder than ever to overtake on a tight circuit. Unfortunately I lost time early on fighting with Nick Heidfeld and damaged my front wing running over a kerb. Just after our planned pit stop, as a result of which I lost more time because I had to have a new nose fitted, it began to rain, so I had to come in again to switch to wets. Ralf was running eighth and I was playing catch-up when he tangled with Villeneuve after an ambitious overtaking move by the Canadian backfired. I was very pleased afterwards when I discovered that I had been lapping as fast as Michael Schumacher, who won, during the wet part of the race because I needed some consolation news like that after finishing eleventh.

We were closer to the target with the FW22s when the circus moved on to Magny-Cours for the French Grand Prix in July. Ralf got a little more out of his car during qualifying to take fifth place, but I was satisfied with the final place in the top ten. We were still having to run less wing, which reduces drag, to try to compensate for the reduction in horsepower, but we had begun to make progress again with the car, which was encouraging. I didn't make a particularly brilliant start and lost a position to Johnny Herbert on the opening lap, but then I passed Eddie Irvine and Mika Salo and went on to finish eighth. The team decided that Ralf had the better chance here, so they brought me in sooner for my second stop. I was running right behind him at the time, but I could see the sense of their plan, even though it was going to jeopardize my chances of scoring points. By staying out longer he was able to fight clear of Frentzen and to finish ahead of Trulli. I got stuck behind Frentzen as a result of my earlier second stop, and finished right on his tail.

Things went back into alarm mode after qualifying for the race in Austria on 16 July. The A1-Ring is a funny little place because the track is a different colour to most circuits, but it's nice and fast and wide, and very smooth as well. I liked it, but the FW22s didn't. We just couldn't find a decent balance, and I lined up eighteenth following major set-up problems all through the Saturday. Nonetheless, I felt I was making progress. But then the engine broke in my race car, so I had to switch to the spare. Without that, I think another top ten was more than likely. Ralf was a place behind me on the grid, scratching his head as he went a different route on set-up. It was clear that we were both struggling again in the low-speed corners, and on the low-grip surface, but part of that was because we had to run the harder Bridgestone tyre option because we simply got too much understeer on the softer rubber. The cars just didn't seem to work so well there, but this time I got more out of mine than Ralf did out of his.

As it happened, for once starting so far back was an advantage. At the start Michael Schumacher was slow away and got hit from behind by Ricardo Zonta in the first corner. All hell broke loose. Schumacher, Trulli and Fisichella found themselves out of the race; a lot of other drivers lost time trying to avoid debris and spinning cars. I, however, was able to nip through into sixth place before the safety car came out to hold us in order until things were cleared up.

When the race went green again I lost a couple of places, but subsequently regained one and was in seventh place after my fuel stop. Herbert and Salo ahead of me still had to make theirs, so when they refuelled I moved up to fifth and finished the race there. Unfortunately Villeneuve managed to leapfrog us all, but I finished right on his tail after a slight off-track moment on the fifty-third lap. I was really pleased to salvage two valuable points from a race that had looked hopeless, and to have got my campaign back on track after the lean spell. My fifth place also put the team back into third place in the constructors' race.

As I reflected on my first half-season in Formula One, the driving side of things was precisely what I had expected it to be. I knew it would be hard racing against the best drivers in the world, but I felt I was coping well with that challenge. But off the circuit it was very difficult to know what to expect because so much of the sport is about politics. In that respect I'd had some good times and some bad times. If nothing else, I think I'd given the media plenty of copy. It was just a shame that it wasn't always for the right reasons.

Things were definitely looking up, though. Since the Montoya speculation had surfaced, no fewer than five teams had expressed an interest in my services for 2001: Benetton, Jaguar, Jordan, BAR and Prost. Given that, I felt confident that I would not be a one-shot wonder. It was simply a matter of determining which offer was the best for my long-term career.

TEN

GIVING IT LARGE

The 2000 German Grand Prix at the end of July remains the best result of my Formula One career to date, so not surprisingly I have fond memories of that race. I'd driven the very high-speed Hockenheim track back in my Formula Ford days and won there, so I moved on to Germany full of optimism after my fifth place in Austria. I thought I was getting back into a good rhythm, and to make things better still BMW had a new engine for us, which gave us back the power that had been trimmed off in the interests of reliability.

Things got off to a promising start when I was seventh fastest in free practice on Friday, only a second slower than Mika Hakkinen in the McLaren, who was fastest. On a circuit where it could stretch its legs, our car felt great. That left me feeling very encouraged for qualifying, but that turned out to be a disaster. I was confident I could qualify sixth or seventh, but I ended up sixteenth. Ralf was fourteenth, in the same boat. The trouble was that the conditions were changeable, and we just didn't time things right. I was bitterly disappointed.

If I thought that was bad, however, it was nothing compared to my start. I was sitting on the grid ready for the formation lap, and suddenly my engine just cut out. That meant I had to start at the back, and even then I made a crap start, which left me trailing Jean Alesi's Prost for ages before I could find a way by. But this was one of those weird races. It started in the sun, then there was a bit of drizzle and then a lot of rain along with some thunder and some lightning, and at one point some nutter was wandering along the side of the track. And it still turned out to be the best race of my career! Even when I was chasing Jean I could feel just how good the car was, and I was relaxed. I had never felt so on top of my job. It was a wonderful feeling, and if that's what Michael feels so often, no wonder he has no thoughts about retiring just yet.

I became aware of the figure in a plastic raincoat walking down the side of the track near the Jim Clark chicane around the twenty-fourth lap. It transpired that he was a Frenchman who had a grudge against Mercedes-Benz, who had sacked him not long before. He had hoped to disrupt the French Grand Prix nearly a month before, without success, and had been turned away from the gate leading to the start line at Hockenheim only hours earlier. As he wandered up and down, the safety car was deployed until he could be brought in. That worked a little in my favour, though I was still only eighteenth when the safety car left the track.

I made my pit stop immediately, on the twenty-sixth lap, but then, on the thirtieth lap, the safety car was called out again after an accident involving Diniz and Alesi. Now I was up to tenth, and no sooner had we started racing again than it began to rain on parts of the circuit. The team called me in for wets on the thirty-fourth lap, and I was the first of those who swapped tyres to do so. Out at the front Rubens Barrichello stayed on drys and went on to win.

In our case the tyre call was a good one, more than making up for our delay in stopping at the Nürburgring. Suddenly I began to move up as other people decided that wet tyres were the way to go. The car still felt brilliant, and I was able to lean really hard on it. I had never enjoyed driving a Formula One car so much, it was just fantastic. Before long I was up to sixth, then fifth, and I could see Mika Salo ahead of me struggling as his tyres lost their edge. I was able to close in and snatch fourth place from him with just two laps to go. That was a major thrill. Hockenheim is a scary old place in the wet at the speeds we drive, but it was a fabulous race for me. Apart from my problem on the formation lap, I enjoyed every second of it.

I was delighted for Rubens, too. He'd been waiting so long for his first win that he burst into tears on the podium. I know how it felt to drive round there that day on wets, so to have finished the race on drys was just fantastic. He really deserved the top spot.

I got another nice little boost later that week. At Hockenheim David, Harald and I had had further talks with Flavio Briatore at Benetton, and with Craig Pollock at BAR and Peter Sauber about possible drives in 2001. Then Niki Lauda voiced his view that Williams should have kept me instead of signing Montoya. 'I don't understand why Williams wanted to replace him,' Niki said. 'He's done a good job this year, they have invested in him, and to me it is probably a bigger gamble to run Montoya.' Which was nice!

The Hungarian Grand Prix on 13 August was less inspirational, although the meeting started well enough. Hard work by the team had brought about a big improvement in the car's behaviour on slow corners; the Hungaroring has plenty of them and requires the same maximum downforce that we run at Monaco. We had a better engine, the team had developed greater downforce, and we were getting the hang of setting the cars up, so we were moving in the right direction again. Ralf qualified fourth using the new qualifying engine, and I was eighth without it, just three tenths behind him.

I was pretty pleased with that, especially as I'd never seen the place before and it can be quite a tricky circuit despite its low-speed nature. Unfortunately, my race was not up to the same level. I was fighting for sixth place when my engine cracked an exhaust and left me powerless to resist late challenges from Trulli and Irvine, which pushed me down to a ninth-place finish.

Before we moved on to Belgium, David and Harald agreed terms with Flavio Briatore for me to move to Benetton-Renault for two years to partner Giancarlo Fisichella. It was a relief after all the speculation and uncertainty to know exactly what I would be doing the following year. But before I left BMW Williams I was determined to show them just what I could do.

Of all the tracks on which we race, Spa Francorchamps in Belgium's foresty Hautes Fagnes region is one of my absolute favourites. I'd raced there before, in Formula Ford and in Formula Three, and I was really looking forward to driving a Formula One car there. But even I never expected to outqualify Michael Schumacher there. If Hockenheim was my best race up to that point, Spa remains my best ever qualifying performance.

I was second fastest to Hakkinen on the Friday, just three tenths of a second off the McLaren. That was a great boost, and that form continued on Saturday morning. In the afternoon I had one of the new qualifying engines in the back of my car and made best use of it. The car felt brilliant again; sweeping through Eau Rouge flat out was mind-blowing. It got to the stage where I decided not to make any further changes to the set-up, instead just to fine-tune my own limits. I kept chipping away, and with nine minutes of the session to go I set my best time. I was two hundredths of a second shy of my first front-row start, and only Hakkinen and Trulli were faster. The icing on the cake was that Michael Schumacher, alongside me in fourth spot, was a tenth slower still. Ralf was sixth.

It took a while for it to sink in that I'd outqualified the driver I rated highest. I certainly hadn't been expecting to go *that* well, especially as my car had a problem with its power-steering that made corners such as Blanchimont a real struggle just to hold on. But overall the car was sensational, so it was just a case of me pushing myself as hard as I could without going off. Gerhard Berger saw the irony in the fact that I'd just completed my Benetton deal, saying to the media, 'I'm sure we are going to get him back from Benetton even better than he is now.' I saw Frank later in the garage, and he had a big beaming smile on his face. 'Not bad for a schoolboy,' was his comment. I felt on top of the world. I even got to go to the post-qualifying press conference for the first time.

It rained on race day, Sunday 27 August, but even during the morning warm-up the car felt great and I was third fastest behind Mika and Michael. Because it was still wet the organizers took the decision to start us in single file behind the safety car. That was a shame, because I'm sure I could have made a good start and gained ground, although had I been down the back of the grid I'd probably have thought otherwise. Hakkinen led us round, then we started racing, and immediately I felt that Trulli was holding me up. He was four seconds slower than Hakkinen in the early laps, and having opened up a gap over Michael I could see the red nose of the Ferrari quickly getting back within striking distance. I was pretty annoyed, even more so when Michael got me at the Bus Stop chicane at the end of the third lap after my own challenge on Trulli had failed to come off. It was no disgrace to be overtaken by the world champion-elect, but you never want to give away a place to anyone, especially when the guy in front is holding you up.

Going down to the La Source hairpin on the next lap, Michael pulled ahead of Jarno and I saw a gap and dived for the inside. Unfortunately it was one of those that closed as I got to it, and we made contact. The Jordan spun and I lost places to David Coulthard and Ralf on the run down to Eau Rouge.

I spent the next couple of laps just checking that the collision hadn't hurt my car, then began to press on again. Later I got to fourth spot after Coulthard lost ground as a result of his pit stop, but in the closing stages he caught and passed me again. I was pleased with my third fifth-place finish of the season, but also disappointed. Without that incident with Trulli I'm sure I would have had a shot at my first podium finish. Somebody wrote after that race that if you are quick at Spa you are a real racing driver, so I guess I had proved something to the people who had got fed up with all the hype over my graduation to Formula One at the beginning of the year. After the race we were able to watch on video the move Hakkinen pulled at Les Combes to lap Zonta on the inside and overtake Michael just as Michael was overtaking Zonta on the outside. That was pretty cool!

I should have notched up some more points at Monza on 10 September, but this time it was Michael who stymied my chances. After Spa, qualifying at Monza was a real let-down. For some reason the FW22 developed an abnormal sensitivity to rises in temperature. Ralf and I would set up our cars in cooler conditions, only to find ourselves losing pace as the ambient temperature went up. It was all to do with tyre temperatures: as they rose, we lost speed. And it was pretty hot at Monza when it mattered on Saturday afternoon. I decided to take off the downforce for qualifying, but paid the price as the car slid about and raised the tyre temperatures even more. Ralf qualified seventh, I was twelfth. Not for the first time, I felt very frustrated.

For a while in the race, though, things looked more promising. The start at Monza is always a big deal, because you blast off the line and reach a good speed before having to brake very heavily for the first chicane. Almost inevitably, there was a collision there involving the Saubers and Irvine's Jaguar. But when we got to the second chicane all hell broke loose. The Jordans of Frentzen and Trulli got tangled up, and Coulthard's McLaren and Barrichello's Ferrari were the innocents who got caught up in the mêlée. Then de la Rosa went barrel-rolling into the gravel bed as well, after hitting the back of Herbert's Jaguar.

The safety car was deployed while the damaged cars were moved away, and as we circulated behind it I was in sixth place behind Schumacher, Hakkinen, Villeneuve, Ralf and Fisichella. We went on like that for ten and a half laps, at which point Michael put me off on the back straight. He was pacing us, as the leader, and coming out of Ascari he slowed down, which is normal. But then he accelerated hard and braked very hard. Everyone in the five-car group behind him got caught out. It was a case of me being the one with no track left to lose. The others were lucky. I wasn't. I had to swerve to avoid a collision with Villeneuve, and with cars spread across the circuit as a result of Michael's actions I ended up on the grass and swiped the guardrail. That damaged a wheel, so for me it was game over. I was pretty annoyed later when somebody accused me of overtaking under the safety car. After Jacques had to stand on the brakes to avoid overtaking those in front of him, I had nowhere to go but the grass.

This incident of course paled into insignificance when I learned later that a marshal, Paolo Ghislimberti, had been killed in the accident at the second chicane. He was hit by a wheel from one of the Jordans. That was the first time I'd ever been exposed to death at a race track, and it affected me big time. I'd never even so much as been in the same area as someone who got killed. Never. It was pretty scary. I didn't see the entire accident, only part of it as I threaded my way through the debris. But it was very sad, especially as Paolo wasn't being paid to be there, he was just doing his job for fun, out of enthusiasm for motorsport. But when you get in the car you must close off your mind to such thoughts. That's sometimes the hard part of our sport: having to carry on.

The next stop was Indianapolis, and Formula One's first visit to America for nine years. That made the US Grand Prix a race on which a great deal hung. Formula One needs to be in the United States, so it was crucial that the event went well.

I loved the place from the moment I saw it. America is cool, and the people at the Indianapolis Motor Speedway had moved heaven and earth to come up with a spectacular facility. The Grand Prix circuit uses a lot of the famous banked oval that holds the Indianapolis 500 each May, although we run in the opposite direction. We go through Turn One the wrong way – it was a gas running on the banking even if it was just another flat-out corner – then turn off part of the way down the front straight to negotiate an infield section before rejoining the oval just before its Turn Two.

The car was running really well for me all weekend, and the balance was fantastic. I felt I could do anything with it. I was fourth quickest on Friday and second quickest to Hakkinen in the damp on Saturday morning. It felt like Spa all over again. I was being much more assured, much less tentative than I had been in similar circumstances earlier in the season, and I found myself praying for a wet race. Qualifying was dry, and I was pleased enough when I set the sixth fastest time, but I really had thought something better than that was possible. Unfortunately my third run was ruined when Alesi blew his engine, and on my fourth I spoiled things in Turn One by sliding wide as the team was urging me to push really hard. That put me on the third row alongside my sparring partner at Spa, Jarno Trulli.

Race day was pretty spectacular. I'd never seen anything like it. The official crowd figure was 250,000, and I could well believe it. There were people everywhere, and just like the fans at home and in Italy they seemed incredibly knowledgeable and enthusiastic. I was hoping I'd be able to give them something to remember.

There was something about Jarno and me at that time, like we had a magnetic attraction to each other. At the start I got away well on wet tyres on a greasy track and retained my sixth place, but again I felt that Jarno was holding me up. I put my hand up for the Spa incident, but this one was down to him. I got alongside him in the infield on the second lap, but he came across on the straight when I was almost through and closed the door. That delayed us both, because I picked up a puncture and lost a load of time crawling back to the pits and ended up in the gravel. The track was drying out so I was one of the first to switch from wet to dry tyres, and I was pretty stoked up and really giving it one. I was hoping I might still be able to retrieve the situation, the way I had at Hockenheim. In twelve laps I managed to go from twenty-first to eighth, trading fastest laps with Michael, but then the engine died after running over the famous strip of bricks on the start/finish line and my race was over on the fifteenth lap. I wasn't very happy, especially as I had been alongside Barrichello on the straight fighting for seventh place. Afterwards I heard that Jarno thought I was an idiot who needed to cool down. As far as I was concerned he needed to think before turning into a space that was already occupied by another car. I put our score at one all.

The Japanese Grand Prix was my most consistent and satisfying race meeting. Everyone went there at the beginning of October focused on the World Championship battle between Michael Schumacher and Mika Hakkinen – Michael had eighty-eight points to Mika's eighty going into the race – but I was mentally

TOP: A lot of drivers dislike the frequent press conferences at races, but I was delighted to address the media after qualifying third on the grid for the Belgian GP at Spa in August 2000.

Sutton Motorsport Images

MIDDLE: The early laps at Spa were exhilarating as I led Michael Schumacher, David Coulthard and Ralf Schumacher round one of the toughest tracks in the world.

Sutton Motorsport Images

BOTTOM: Trulli spins after we make contact at Spa's La Source hairpin, as Ralf Schumacher takes avoiding action and David Coulthard slips down the inside of me.

Sutton Motorsport Images

ABOVE: That's me on the grass at Monza just before the restart of the 2000 Italian GP, after Michael Schumacher brake-tested the leading bunch as we ran behind the safety car. I lost any chance of a top six result as I was forced to take avoiding action and swiped the barrier. Sutton Motorsport Images

BELOW: A lot of people wondered where my career was going at Monaco in 2000. Here at the Loews hairpin Pedro de la Rosa blocks the track as I wait with Nick Heidfeld, Pedro Diniz and Mark Gene for the track to be cleared. Eventually the race was red-flagged and restarted. Sutton Motorsport Images

ABOVE: The Japanese GP of 2000 was my most satisfying Formula One outing to date, as I finished fifth in the BMW Williams behind the two Ferraris and McLarens after out-qualifying and out-racing my team-mate Ralf Schumacher on a circuit every bit as challenging as Spa. Sutton Motorsport Images

ABOVE: I've always been a big fan of computer games. Playing with my Sony PlayStation is a great way to relax.

Sutton Motorsport Images

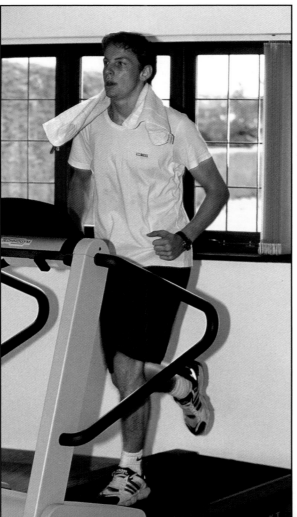

LEFT: Fitness is a key part of a racing driver's life. I do a mixture of disciplines, including swimming, weights and running, both outdoors and indoors.

Sutton Motorsport Images

ABOVE: I met Louise Griffiths in September 2000, and she has become one of the most important people in my life. We are both ambitious, and she is as supportive of my racing as I am of her music career.
Button Family

ABOVE RIGHT: On my 21st birthday in 2001, with the two most important women in my life: Louise on my right, and my mum, Simone, on my left. We had a ball.
Andrea Wright/CAN International © 2001

RIGHT: I have a great relationship with my three sisters (from left) Natasha, Samantha and Tanya. Andrea Wright/CAN International © 2001

As we had expected, the early races in 2001 were a real struggle for Benetton Renault. Here at Imola I finished twelfth after a refuelling rig problem in the San Marino GP. LAT

More than once my racing in 2001 ended by the side of the track with a blown engine, but it was a year in which we laid the solid foundation for a strong challenge this season.

Bearne/Sutton Motorsport Images

I had some interesting conversations in 2001 with Benetton chief Flavio Briatore, but our relationship grew stronger as the year progressed and we are pushing ahead with great optimism this year. Sutton Motorsport Images

The German GP at Hockenheim signalled the turning point for me in 2001. The car was much more competitive and I scored my first points of the season with fifth place.

Oops! At the first corner chicane at Monza I have already lost the nose wing from my Benetton Renault as I head Coulthard and the Jaguars of Irvine and de la Rosa.

I'm pleased to say that I've always had good relationships with my team-mates. I was chuffed that Ralf Schumacher came to congratulate me after my result at Hockenheim, where he had just won for BMW Williams. That's Enrique Bernoldi between us.

I had a really strong race in Japan to end 2001, finishing seventh behind the dominant Ferrari, McLaren and BMW Williams teams. That's the Suzukaland rollercoaster in the background as I speed through the demanding Dunlop curves behind the pits. Steven Tee/LAT preparing myself for the toughest and most exhilarating circuit on the calendar. Suzuka has a bit of everything, from the dauntingly fast esses at the beginning of the lap to the two maximum-commitment Dunlop left-handers behind the pits, a hairpin, the fast and sweeping Spoon Curve and the long haul to the fast 130R left-hander and the final chicane. There's even a crossover, just like my old Scalextric track! It's not one of those tracks you can learn instantly. There's just too much to focus on. It's one of those places where you have to build up your speed, piecing the whole lap together in stages. I've found subsequently that it takes me more laps to get into a drive at Suzuka than any other circuit.

By the Friday night I was a second and a half off Ralf, but I picked up a lot of time on Saturday as I found my rhythm. That might have had something to do with a good night's sleep. Usually I acclimatize quickly to any new place, but I had really bad jet lag in Japan, and Friday night was the first time I really got my head down. I was third fastest in the morning, and in qualifying I finished fifth, the fastest car outside the McLarens and Ferraris. Yet again the car felt superb. I was surprised to be so quick, because my first run was inadvertently spoiled by Mika Hakkinen and then Trulli got in the way on the second. My third run was the best. As I left the pits for it I told the team over the radio, 'I'm going to give it large, boys.' I couldn't resist. After that I waited for somebody to beat my time. They did, as Ralf improved to fifth place. But I was able to go out again and take the position back. I was very chuffed to find that I was faster than Michael through the esses – fastest of all, in fact.

It was damp for the start of the race and I made a lousy getaway. As Ralf catapulted up to fourth I fell back to seventh behind Eddie Irvine. I just overheated the clutch and was still looking for the bite point as everyone started coming past. But the car was as good as it had been in qualifying and I was able to hunt him and Ralf down and move back up to fifth place. I was closing on Rubens Barrichello at the finish, but on a day when the two Ferraris and the two McLarens were dominant, and Michael Schumacher became Ferrari's first world champion since Jody Scheckter in 1979, that was the best I could hope for.

A lot of fuss was made about the fact that I had outqualified Ralf on the three real drivers' circuits – Interlagos, Spa and Suzuka – but I had a great relationship with him when we could have had an edgy time together. It was always difficult to talk with him, but then everyone found it difficult to talk to him. I don't know why that was, I can't say. Maybe because that's just the way he is. A case of I'm more experienced and I've been here longer, perhaps. You can speak to me but I'm not going to speak to you. That sort of thing. So to start with it was tough and I had to initiate conversations. But when I got quicker he actually began to respect me more, which was good, and we got on really well. Towards the end of the year I was outqualifying him more than he was outqualifying me, and still we got on really well. Maybe just after qualifying he wouldn't be happy, but then half an hour later he'd say, 'Well done.' It was good to be competitive with someone like Ralf, to push him to the limit, because I'd always watched him on TV and everyone was saying that he was going to be the Next Big Thing. As he showed in 2001, there's still a good chance of that.

Jenson was fantastic in the race at Hockenheim, fantastic in qualifying at Spa. Indianapolis was a strong performance. At Suzuka he was very, very strong. In the second half of the season he was good everywhere, really. He was unlucky, but lucky. He was lucky that he

got the chance in the first place, unlucky that ultimately there was someone else in the bus queue.

Jim Wright, Head of Marketing, Williams F1 team

I was really hoping to round off my first season with another strong finish in the final race, in Malaysia, but things didn't work out that way. The Sepang circuit proved a very tricky one to set the car up for, and though I was as quick as Ralf in practice I lost track time on Saturday morning with an hydraulic failure on the qualifying engine I was planning to use. That left me with a less powerful unit for qualifying, and I struggled a bit on my way to sixteenth place on the grid. The problem also prevented me scrubbing in front tyres. When you do that you just take the initial shine off the tread area and bring the tyres to the point where they will work at peak efficiency. With my tyres unscrubbed, I was struggling all through the session to get the car balanced. We were, to tell the truth, all at sea. I managed to climb as high as tenth place by the nineteenth lap of the race, but then the engine broke.

It was a horrible way to sign off, but I felt proud to have helped BMW Williams to third place in the Constructors Championship. Ralf recorded three third-place podium finishes in the most impressive Formula One début for an all-new engine since the Ford Cosworth DFV arrived in 1967. Overall we had fourteen top-six finishes and scored thirty-six World Championship points, as Ralf and I met the chequered flag eighteen times from thirty-four starts. Ralf had five accidents and I had one, he had four mechanical retirements due to failures on the car and I had two, and I had five engine failures. We used six FW22 chassis and two hundred BMW V10s during the seventeen races and completed some nineteen thousand kilometres of testing, developing not just a new car but also a new engine.

The first year of our partnership with BMW presented many challenges and various technical difficulties. But the year was very constructive for the future and perhaps we were even more successful than we had expected.

Ralf once again demonstrated his remarkable talent, and the significant number of points he scored for the team and his fifth place in the World Championship clearly confirmed his success. He completed his fourth Formula One season and was able to offer lots of helpful experience.

Jenson was really the discovery of the year – I don't think anybody would deny that. He was very popular in the team, and both his driving talent and his potential spoke for themselves.

Frank Williams

Jenson was excellent. He probably had a few more engine problems than Ralf in the first part of the season, but he proved a quick learner and he adapted well to unfamiliar new circuits. He really rose to the challenge. I suppose, in short, you could say that he was perfect.

Patrick Head, Technical Director, Williams F1 team

I can't think of a new driver in Formula One who made so few mistakes in his first season.

Gerhard Berger, BMW Motorsport

I think Jenson's first year of Formula One completely lived up to the expectations I had of him after the test he did with Prost in December 1999. I think he did very well. It's difficult to comment on other people's engineering staff, but I think he did a very good job, though possibly

below what I expected he would. I expected him to do more of a Montoya, to actually be up there straight away and get some podiums straight away. But I don't know the full ins and outs, and the second half of his year was certainly pretty impressive for a rookie.

Humphrey Corbett, Prost race engineer

Just after Christmas, I got another present. This one came from no less a personality than Michael Schumacher, the newly crowned world champion and one of the Formula One figures I had most admired during the formative years of my career. He was quoted as saying that he believed I would improve on my 'excellent début season with BMW Williams'. 'People were critical when they heard Jenson Button was arriving in Formula One without much experience,' he continued. 'But I was always under the impression that if someone is able to go in the car and be fast immediately and doesn't crash, then he has the talent and right to be in Formula One. Jenson proved to be fast immediately, he didn't crash very often. He made very few mistakes. Simply, he is one of the future stars.' I wasn't going to argue with that.

At the end of my first season I was still pretty much the same guy I'd been at the start. I'd learned a lot of things, and of course running with the big boys had helped me to mature as a driver, but I was still ironing my own shirts at home. I'd weathered all the complaints about the hype my rapid graduation had given rise to, and the criticisms of David and Harald for whipping it up. The truth is they did a great job for me because they were enthusiastic and they believed in me. The media then just got hold of the story and ran with it. It was hardly my management's fault.

Dad was right when he said, just after Frank had told me I had got the drive, that the world would be completely different when we got home. But I think I kept my feet on the ground, and in my first season in Formula One I hope I justified some of the faith people had in me.

ELEVEN

THE RIGHT STUFF

A lot of guys dream of becoming Formula One drivers because they've just driven their Peugeot 205 GTi at 120mph down the M1. Sorry, fellas, but it doesn't work that way. The average road car driver would last about two laps, maybe three, if they were taken at racing speed in a Formula One car. Believe me, it's a different world.

My Renault B202 accelerates from rest to 60mph in 2.5 seconds, and hits 200mph in less than ten. It corners in excess of 3g and brakes at more than 5g. That means every time I go round a corner I weigh 223.5kg instead of 74.5kg, and every time I brake really hard I weigh 372.5kg. Try doing that round a track like Monte Carlo for nearly two hours in a Grand Prix and you'll appreciate that it's like nothing you've ever experienced before.

The steering is very heavy, even with power-steering. It's not like driving your road car. Our Michelin tyres are super-grippy. Also, the throttle isn't the softest thing and you've got to hit the brakes as hard as you can every corner. You're always moving, there's never any time to rest, even during a pit stop. You're constantly working. Long-distance drives really take it out of you cardio-vascularly, because you are working so hard. Mentally it takes it out of you too, because things happen so fast that you've got to react to them in a way you wouldn't normally have to. When you're physically fit it helps you mentally too. You recover faster and your reactions are better.

One of the reasons we are paid so much money to drive these cars is that we are sad men who hide ourselves away from the rest of humanity for great chunks of our time, working ourselves like mice on a treadmill in the gymnasiums of the world. You really do have to be very fit, or you simply aren't going to last. Teams are not going to invest millions of dollars developing the world's fastest cars, then turn them over to wimps with spaghetti arms who get knackered after ten laps.

At Renault Sport we have a great Human Performance Centre, managed by Bernie Shrosbee. I work with him, and also train regularly with Hogne Rorvik, who has two degrees, in chiropractic and sports physiotherapy. He attends our training camps and keeps me in good order at the races. Besides being my personal physio, he's a good and loyal friend too. I also benefit from the talents of Phil 'The Monk' Young, who has a private sports therapy practice and works with Renault during the season. In 2001 he helped me by doing a lot of work on my back. He's like something out of *Austin Powers* – Dr Evil, with the 'lazor'. The exercises I do improve my stamina and my cardio-vascular performance. They are very basic but very important. I also do weight training, to improve my upper body strength.

The other important exercise, of course, is driving the car. You can do all the weight training, running and gym work you like, and all of that is crucial, but in the final analysis the thing that trains you best for driving Formula One cars is driving Formula One cars. Hogne doesn't believe that you can do fitness exercises that truly imitate the experience of actually driving the car. To train the specific group of muscles you use when driving a Formula One car, and to get your body used to the g forces, you have to get out there and drive. That's mainly because of the need to get your neck muscles used to their task. But you can't sit in the car all the time, so you need to add strength in other ways. And it's not so much power strength you need as endurance strength.

Speed is down to talent. Like balance and co-ordination, it's innate. You're either born with it or you aren't. But Hogne believes you can train that too, so we do neuro-muscular training, which is all about honing the nerves in your muscular system. Everyone has loads of receptors in their muscles, joints and tendons. The way in which a muscle responds to any sudden change of position, for example, is the result of how many receptors react and how the information goes through your central nervous system and out again. So that's a trainable system. A good neuro-muscular set-up helps balance, co-ordination and spatial awareness.

I don't know how many other drivers do neuro-muscular training. Hogne and I use balance boards. Research has shown that these wobble boards are very good for sports injuries. They are also a good way to optimize the neuro-muscular functions in your back and neck. How can a big guy lift a cup of coffee and twinge his back? It's exactly the same thing when you have an ankle distortion. It's just a misfiring; for a thousandth of a second the system doesn't work in your spinal column. Wobble-board training helps to prevent those sorts of malfunctions by training the nerves. I'll sit on a wobble board and maintain my stability, then Hogne will throw balls at me, or he'll stand behind me and push to upset the equilibrium. The trick is to resist the forces that are trying to upset you, and to maintain the equilibrium. It's good training for the reflexes. It demands great concentration, but it's definitely beneficial.

Jenson hadn't done much training before Formula One. He wasn't really unfit, though. He had been karting since he was eight, so that had given him some fitness for racing. He'd done some swimming and cycling and some weight training, but not very much.

You can't just train three or four hours a day. That would just destroy you. It would have a very negative effect on your body. So you have to sort of rush slowly. The first year in Formula One I was not unhappy with him. The main goal was to make him like training and feel comfortable, and to feel the need for physical training. That's done. Now he enjoys it. I would say that took a year. He didn't always do it happily, sometimes it was a pain in the arse! Throughout the season there was a big change, though, and also through the winter of 2000/01. There was a training camp right after New Year in Lanzarote, and he really began enjoying it. After that it's been fine.

If Michael Schumacher is 100 per cent, there is definitely still very big potential for Jenson. I would say that to begin with he was maybe 50 per cent. By the end of 2000 we had got maybe another 10 per cent, and at the beginning of 2001 he was up to 65. I think we need another one and a half years to bring him up to Michael's level. Michael is very fit, I think, from everything that I have heard, read and seen. To get to that level takes more than two or three years. I think Jenson can reach 80, 90 per cent of that level in two years from the start of this new season.

Hogne Rorvik, personal physiotherapist

My fitness when I came into Formula One was okay, but I agree with Hogne when he says I hit 65 per cent of Michael's level by the beginning of 2001. Now I think I'm way above that percentage mark. I trained every day for months during 2001, whenever I was able to. Today, in the winter of 2001/02, I'm 100 per cent happy with my fitness. To begin with, in my BMW Williams days, it was very difficult. I didn't have a training camp or trainers pushing me to do stuff. Now at Renault I do, and it's great. I never liked training. I'd always do it, but I never liked it. But when Bernie Shrosbee came along he made it so much more interesting. We'd all train together and it was great. Now I love it, and I can feel the difference.

The fitness programme we have at Renault is six days a week, ninety minutes a day minimum, and on average in the racing season we manage to do that. At the end of the season there's a training camp for four to seven days every month, November through to February, but that focuses only on physical training. In the off season you do as much training as possible. Hogne and I do six days a week.

Cardio-vascularly I'm very fit, although I've still got work to do on my upper body because of the shoulder problem I had early in 2001 as a result of which I had to start taking it a bit easy. I think the cause was a combination of the car being really heavy to drive, without power-steering, and movement in the little joint between my collarbone and shoulder. There was slightly more movement in one side than the other – not by a big margin, it was just that one side was a bit slacker. The extra load needed to drive the car allied to this slight slackness led eventually to an inflammation in the joint, which in turn led to a strained shoulder. There were muscular reactions as well, and I struggled with those for a few weeks too.

It was, however, 100 per cent treatable. Hogne began to apply an anti-inflammatory preparation, but because of my schedule the shoulder never really got enough rest. The problem went on and on, so we decided to see a specialist to confirm the original diagnosis and get a cortisone injection. But he didn't agree with that treatment. He thought the muscles were the main problem and refused us the injection. That delayed my recovery for weeks, until finally we went to another specialist, at a hospital in England, who used ultrasound and a scan to confirm the original diagnosis. I eventually received a cortisone injection in the joint and within five days the shoulder had improved dramatically. It's been fine ever since.

It wasn't really a massive problem – we contained it by doing more training to compensate for the slackness and prevent a recurrence – and I don't think it affected my performances too much, but it was certainly painful by the end of a race. Unfortunately the whole thing got blown up out of all proportion in May 2001 between the Spanish and Monaco Grands Prix and there was all sorts of speculation flying around that I was going to be stood down or replaced. Well, if a driver had a shoulder injury that made it dangerous for him to race, fair enough. But it wasn't that bad. It might hurt a lot, but it wasn't going to cause a terminal problem if I put it through a race, so I carried on. No reason to stop. I suppose that, if anything, that situation underlines why Formula One drivers need to maintain ultimate fitness.

In 2001 I really started to believe Hogne when he said that the fitter you are, the better you are on the track. Now it's my credo too. You don't have to have the lung capacity of an Olympic long-distance runner. There are physical and mental resources that are more important in motorsport, such as concentration, attitude, breathing. Breathing is all part of cardio-vascular fitness. The rate at which your heart beats while driving is not really representative of the physical work you're doing. It's dominated by emotional reactions, adrenalin and other things the body produces that are largely if not completely beyond your control. The fitter you are, obviously the better your heart and pulse rates are. My average pulse in the car is 140, whereas my rest pulse is below fifty. Normal people are between sixty and seventy at rest. Those figures would be way up if they were in a moving Formula One car.

What can limit your performance is bad regulation of body temperature and loss of bodily fluids. They can cause problems, especially during races when the ambient temperature is high. It's difficult to drink in the car. Some drivers drink only half a litre, and even though there are salts in the drink to help replace bodily fluids, that's way too little. You can easily lose two to three litres during a race. So through temperature regulation and by using a better system for drinking, you can improve your performance quite a bit towards the end of the race. If a person who weighs 70kg loses three litres of bodily fluids, his performance will definitely go down at least 15 to 20 per cent. It's difficult to measure the effect of that on concentration, but there will be one, although a high level of cardio-vascular fitness will help combat a decrease in mental alertness. The limit is around three litres; if you lose more than that it will definitely adversely affect your concentration and physical performance. That could cost you a race. I'm lucky because I don't sweat much. In fact, I think I sweat the least among all the Formula One drivers. But how much you sweat is not necessarily an index of how fit you are. It's just an individual thing. Some people sweat more than others, yet they can still be very fit.

At the beginning of my Formula One career I hated running, but I needed to do it. Now I enjoy that too. I do both distance running outside and work on a running machine, but running outside for forty-five to sixty minutes is much more fun. I get bored just staying in the same place. I can get the same training quality out of cycling, and I really enjoy that too, but then I have to double the distance. I'm also careful to vary my pace; sometimes I'm sprinting, sometimes running for endurance. You can't always sustain the same pace all the time. So I'll do a warm-up, then take an interval of rest. The same with cycling, especially when I'm up in the hills around Monaco. I'll do the same with swimming, too: one hour with intervals. Swimming is particularly good cardio-vascular work, but it also exercises all of your muscles in a gentle manner, without the shocks that running can generate. It's a very good way to exercise your whole body, but you need a good technique to make the training valid. Luckily, I'm a pretty good swimmer.

Then there's the gym. I really like the rowing machine because you can work in a good, steady rhythm with that. I also use the weight machine to do butterflies, lat pulls and pull downs, the usual stuff for upper body strength development. I do the bench press too, and dips. All of that focuses on developing the biceps and triceps. When I'm doing strength training I do fifteen to twenty repetitions in four to six series; for power training I use more weight but fewer repetitions, say six to eight. It depends on the specific exercise how much weight I use.

If you were already 100 per cent fit and just seeking the optimum, the ultimate performance, you might look for something more scientifically targeted. But for me it was very simple: we just had to raise the level of my most important physical resources. So there's no reason to be very sophisticated about it. It's not difficult. You just have to do it. It's when you're at world champion level in any sport that you have to be more sophisticated in your training and try to find ways of doing things better than others have done before. I'm going to find out how that feels, believe me.

Neck muscles are also a very important group to train, and it's not hard to see why with all those g forces in cornering and braking a driver must face for up to two hours at a time. In Brazil in my first season I was pretty tired by the end of the race; I had to just relax in the car afterwards, resting my helmet on the Confor foam head-rest. Likewise, at Suzuka that year my arms were screaming after fifteen to twenty laps before the pit stop gave me a bit of a respite. But I was definitely stronger last year, and I'm getting stronger still. It's a great feeling. My advice to any aspiring race driver is to start your physical training well in advance, but take good advice along the way as to what you should be doing.

Another important aspect of driving is energy management in the cockpit, and that's where the cardio-vascular training helps too. The fitter you are, the less energy you have to expend on the pure act of driving. I'm usually very comfortable in the car from that point of view and don't find that I have to expend a lot of energy on driving. If you're fit cardio-vascularly, you'll recover much faster after exercise too. Fifteen minutes after a race I'm usually right back to normal.

When you consider the schedules a driver must face during a typical season, with travel to and from races, practice, qualifying, the races themselves, the fact that you are often back on track test-ing again the Tuesday after a Grand Prix, you can see why we need to be superfit. But all the exercise must be backed up by sufficient sleep and the right personal routine. And, needless to say, because we are athletes we also need to be very careful about what we eat and drink, and when. I've always been careful to avoid weight problems, but eating the right things can also promote fitness.

I eat a lot of carbohydrates: bread, pasta, potatoes. Then there are vegetables and fruit to get the right vitamins, and proteins from meat. I don't eat much red meat, more chicken and fish. It's very important to eat directly after a training session or a race, or as soon as possible. This also helps your ability to recover after exercise.

And you should never eat just before you go to sleep. I drink a lot of water and fruit juice, some tea, not much coffee. At a race meeting it's plenty of water and juices, and during the race itself a special energy drink that isn't particularly strong, but light. I'll drink litres of that during the day. It puts all the salts and minerals that have been sweated out back into the system. If it's too strong, though, your blood sugar level goes up and you get a concentration of insulin, which in turn makes the blood sugar level go down and makes you tired. I have an even weaker concentration drink while I'm racing to avoid the possibility of upsetting my stomach during a race.

I freely admit that I wasn't a great fan of serious fitness training when I first came into Formula One, but now I really enjoy it. It's more than just the flipside of being a racing driver, it's part of my life's routine. I wouldn't want to be without it now. And that's just as well, really, because there's another very pertinent reason why racing drivers need to be superfit. As Martin Donnelly proved after his crash at Jerez in 1990, the fitter you are the better your chances of survival and full recovery after a serious accident.

Formula One can be a funny world. During my first season I was accused by some people of being too soft, of being unable to overtake, although I think I proved my willingness to have a go on several occasions. The same people who said I couldn't race were the first to criticize me for the incident with Jarno Trulli at Spa, when I was trying to do what they said I couldn't. Well, they can't have it both ways.

As for being soft, I think those people need to get into an F1 car and see what it's like. There's no move I could have done in my first year that I didn't do. If you say I'm not aggressive enough, well, I collided with Trulli twice after being too aggressive. Spa was my fault, definitely, but Indianapolis was his. Which is cool. I don't have a problem with aggressiveness at all. That's just people trying to find that something extra.

Driving a Formula One car, let alone actually racing one, is the most exhilarating feeling on earth. It's every good feeling you've ever had multiplied several times. It's like best-ever sex mixed with winning the lottery. It gets your senses flowing and makes you feel totally alive, reacting to the car's every movement. These machines are mega quick, and you drive them on the limit, using every bit of the road. You use an inch too much, though, hit a bit of dust or dirt, and that's enough to shove the whole back end out. You need to be really precise, with your steering, your throttle control and your braking. All your inputs need to be fast but smooth. It's nothing at all like driving a road car. If people had any idea just what these things are like, how far removed they are from their everyday experiences on the country's roads, how tricky they are to drive on the limit, I think they'd really respect the racers, especially when they're braking and performing overtaking manoeuvres. Half the reason overtaking is so rare is that the drivers are so evenly matched. Even when a car is two seconds a lap slower than yours, there are circuits, such as Monaco, where you're going to struggle like mad to pass. Look at the trouble DC had with Enrique Bernoldi at Monaco in 2001.

From the moment I got into a Formula One car I made myself left-foot brake for the first time since my karting days, because in these things that's the quick way to do it. It upsets the car less. And I like a throttle pedal that's soft and has a fair amount of travel. That way you don't have to exert a lot of pressure. I've found that the secret is to make gentle throttle inputs, not to stab at it. You have more control that way. Put your foot down too fast with a Formula One car and you can spin it very easily, although it's slightly less easy these days with traction control. You always want to be on the gas as soon as possible, but you have to use your head, because otherwise you lose traction and get oversteer, and that makes the back of the car step out and wastes time. It's better to have a gradual oversteer that you're creating yourself than for the car to create it as a reaction. Controllable oversteer is the key, particularly in qualifying, but also in racing. So long as you don't have to lift off the gas to get rid of it, that's the way to go.

You feel pretty nervous when you're sitting on the grid prior to the start. You just can't wait to get going; it takes so long for the other cars behind you to line up. That might sound funny, given that at the start of the 2001 season the Benettons were the cars at the back, but it's true. You just want to get going. Everything takes so long. You go into first gear, do what you have to do to get the launch control working, and then you just sit there, waiting. The red lights seem to go out so slowly, and then suddenly it's 200mph time. From everything going too slowly, everything is suddenly happening so quickly. It's such a change, in such a short time. A real adrenalin buzz. The thrill of the speed, the knowledge that you're racing wheel to wheel with the best drivers in the world. There's nothing like it.

And yet I really enjoyed my time in Formula Ford too. I liked the closeness of the racing, which was similar to karting and provided the perfect training ground for the higher categories. You learn a lot of racecraft. But it was a little strange after racing karts abroad. In Formula Ford, whenever you go to pass someone they just seem to block you everywhere. I still can't believe that the authorities don't do more about it. It's a bit like the way people drive in English karting. I can't stand blocking, and I've been told off by one or two teams I've driven for because I won't do it! But in karting I always took the view that if I was fast enough I shouldn't have to do that. If necessary, you let someone by. Then do them again on the next corner.

One of the biggest things karting teaches any driver is how to overtake, which, after all, is one of the most fundamental and important aspects of race driving. I'm sure anyone can learn how to do it. People say it's inbred. Maybe the attitude and willingness is, but you still have to learn the right and the wrong way of doing it. More than anything, though, overtaking is a mentality, and karting teaches you that, especially English karting where most of the time you have three heats. You start one near the front, one in the middle and one down the back regardless of who you are, so you not only learn how to stay ahead of the quick guys, you also learn how to fight your way through from the middle and the back of the field. You learn how to be both offensive and defensive. You are taught all that in karting, but obviously you've got to have the head for it in the first place, the willingness to try and the judgement and spatial awareness to pull it off.

It's the same with the speed; I'm sure you need it in your head to begin with. That's the most fundamental thing of all: you have to be able to drive flat out all the time. You have to have that fundamental need for speed. You never get anywhere by lifting off. The higher up the racing ladder you get, the tougher it is. But it's plenty tough even on the lower slopes. Karting is generally quite well policed, blocking apart, but Formula Ford is pretty much no holds barred. I've never been a believer in blocking and swerving and brake testing, but the odd lunge up the inside of somebody is quite kosher.

That was what I did to Ricardo van der Ende in that European Formula Ford Championship finale at Brands Hatch in 1998: I got alongside him, he turned in on me and I hit him. We both went off. The gap was there when I looked for it, and it closed when I got there. I lost the European Championship because of that – a big mistake. I shouldn't have done it because all I needed to do was finish ahead of my team-mate, but it worked for me at the Formula Ford Festival the following week when I tried it on Marcus Ambrose. Now that's the sort of thing I feel is acceptable, but each driver draws the line in his own way, according to his own moral judgements of what is right and what is wrong.

It's always difficult to comment on famous incidents if you weren't there at the time, but what Ayrton Senna did to Alain Prost at Suzuka in 1990, I would say, was over the top. He had told people the previous day that if Prost got to the first corner ahead of him he wasn't going to let him make it all the way round, and when precisely that happened after the start, he just didn't lift off the throttle and took himself and Prost out of the race by ramming the back of the Frenchman's Ferrari. Early in my Formula One career I was quoted as saying I would take a rival off the track if a championship depended on it. But that isn't quite what I said. I don't agree with deliberately taking another driver off. I think clean driving is good. I've always believed that. But if you're in a possible championship-winning position, or whatever position you are in come to think of it, if there's a move you can try to overtake someone, you're going to try it. Sometimes it works, sometimes it doesn't.

I don't really see anything wrong with what happened between Michael Schumacher and Damon Hill in Adelaide back in 1994, for instance. Just before the incident Michael had gone off the track and hit a wall hard; his Benetton then cut across into the Williams' path as Damon tried to overtake him. It was this controversial move that won him his first world title by a single point. I thought that was OK. Damon didn't have to go for it. He knew the likely consequences.

It's more difficult to make a judgement when you look at the incident between Michael and Jacques Villeneuve at Jerez three years later, when Jacques slid past Michael on the inside going into the first corner and Michael turned into him to try to stop him. I wasn't in the car, and only those two can really comment. But anything from a safe point of view – and it's got to be safe – is on.

Be honest: you're not going to win World Championships by being soft. You've got to be a really, really tough person to be a world champion. Everything's got to be perfect, and you've really got to push. If you come to the last race and it's the last corner and there are two of you who can win the championship and you're together and you're the one who's behind, you're not just going to sit there, are you? You're going to try and get past, and if you end up crashing you end up crashing. So long as it's not a corner where you're doing 200mph and it could be dangerous. But if it's a 40mph corner, you're going to make full use of your resources and attempt to overtake. The stakes are that high these days.

Having said that, I wasn't impressed with what Michael did to me at Monza in 2000 when he virtually brake-tested the field on the back straight just before the restart. When the safety car put its lights out, the signal that it's about to pull off, he slowed down, accelerated hard, then braked really hard. I didn't think that was good. There's nothing in the rules today that says you can't do that – the leader keeps the pace – but I just didn't think that was a good thing to do. He must have known that people behind him had cold brakes because he was braking hard himself to generate heat in his, so something like that was bound to happen. I had to swerve in a hurry and hit the barrier, which ruined my race. The worst part of it was that I very nearly hit a marshal. The guy was standing on the track side of the barrier and I nearly collected him. I was even angrier afterwards when I discovered that a marshal being killed in the incident at the second chicane was the reason why we were under the yellow flag in the first place. Michael apologized later, but I reckon he must have known the possible consequences of what he was doing, with all his experience. I'm not saying he did it on purpose, just that he didn't think about the people behind him. I didn't think it was the right way for a world champion to behave. It happened a few times in 2001, too. Sometimes people up front just don't seem to realize that people behind them have cold brakes.

When you screw up or have a shunt and it's your fault, you go into another world. You've made a mistake and not been able to get any points, and you feel really, really bad. For yourself and for the team, more than anything. But so far as big accidents are concerned, I've been lucky. Apart from my Saturday-morning crunch in Melbourne in March 2000, I haven't had a big one. I've never been upside down in a car, although I did have that shunt at Suzuka in the karting World Cup when I spun after hitting Giorgio Pantano and had to sit there helpless while the rest of the field came hurtling towards me. You don't want to go through that sort of thing too often. But you don't dwell on spins and accidents. You just accept them as part of a racing driver's life and put them out of your mind.

In my brief time in Formula One I have been fortunate to race wheel to wheel with Michael Schumacher and Mika Hakkinen, the top men in the game. And the really weird thing is that I've actually outqualified everyone at some stage except for the Flying Finn. I find that quite strange, although the BMW Williams FW22 was never a match for the Ferrari or the McLaren in 2000. Towards the end of the year it was working much better, but it still wasn't competitive enough, no way. It wasn't a patch on the FW23 Ralf and Montoya raced in 2001.

Of all the guys I've raced against, Michael is easily the most impressive, the best example of a driver with the complete Right Stuff package, with all the ingredients I've mentioned above blended together in the right quantities. It's strange how quite a few drivers treat him differently on the circuit. I think they're intimidated by him. That's one of his plus points, because it helps his confidence big time. I'm not intimidated. All the guys I race against are beatable as far as I'm concerned. They're all human. As early as Brazil in 2000 I felt that I could beat anyone in Formula One. Maybe not in racing, because that's going to take time, but certainly in qualifying. And in the future I'm definitely going to win. After Spa in August 2000 it was like, 'Jesus, I've outqualified everyone here except two people in front of me. My first year in F1!' Then again, if I'd won there or finished second, it would have made everything harder to bear when I was struggling so much with Benetton in the first half of 2001.

TWELVE

HERO TO ZERO

I began work with my new team before the end of the 2000 season, as Frank and Patrick agreed to release me early. Most teams will do this, simply because when everyone starts to move around there isn't much point in holding someone to the final day of a contract. Besides, they took the view that I was only on loan anyway. When we had a goodbye party in the log cabin at Suzuka, Patrick was nice enough to refer to it as a 'welcome back' party.

One of the reasons David and Harald had finally opted for Benetton was that Renault had bought the team. Renault let us see its plans for the future, and they were impressive. The company had first entered Formula One in 1977, when it took the adventurous route of opting for a 1.5-litre turbocharged engine. The rules allowed this, but ever since the three-litre Formula One engine had been introduced in 1966 everyone had always gone for the larger-capacity, normally aspirated engine option. It took Renault to see the benefits of pioneering another route. Eventually, everyone had to have a turbocharged engine. In the new era of 3.5-litre normally aspirated Formula One engines introduced in 1989, Renault's V10 again broke new ground; before long all the V12s and V8s had gone and everyone was using ten cylinders. Renault had also pioneered pneumatic valve actuation, which does away with the need for springs to open and close the valves, instead using pneumatic pressure to enable the engine to rev higher. It's *de rigueur* today.

In 2000 we learned that the company was developing another dramatic departure from the norm. Most V10s in Formula One have narrow angles between the cylinder banks to ensure a small engine profile to tuck onto the rear bulkhead of the chassis. But Renault had re-hired its ace engine designer Jean-Jacques His, and he had come up with a new idea. He widened the V angle so that the engine's, and therefore the car's, centre of gravity was lower. Today's cars are wide enough behind the rear bulkhead so that some extra engine width need not present problems, but a lower centre of gravity can confer significant handling advantages. At the same time, Jean-Jacques was proposing to incorporate in due course some other dramatic new technology. Of course, I'm not going to go into that here. If we have to go through teething troubles with it, I don't see why we should give rivals any clues! Suffice to say that their plans were very encouraging.

In today's Formula One you need to be with a team that at the very least has a partnership with a major engine manufacturer if you are to have any chance of winning races and championships. I'm not in Formula One just to make up the numbers. I want to win, and I want to be world champion. With Renault taking over control of Benetton, I felt I would have the best possible chance of doing that.

One of my first roles was to test with the team's 2000 car, the B200, which used the Supertec V10 that had formerly been the Renault with which Williams and Benetton had won most of the World Championships between 1992 and 1997. We went down to Jerez, and the car felt pretty good, though it was not as good as the BMW Williams I had just been obliged to give up. I had several spins while I was discovering its limits, but nobody seemed unduly worried. I ended the test eleventh fastest, but I was ahead of Ralf Schumacher and Juan Pablo Montoya, which was quite satisfying. I was optimistic for the future. Little did I know what was in store.

Settling into a new team isn't always straightforward, especially when there's another driver who has been there as long as Giancarlo Fisichella had been. He'd come into Formula One in 1996 with Minardi, switched for a year to Jordan, then gone to Benetton in 1998 on the long-term contract he had signed with team chief Flavio Briatore in 1996. So he had his feet well and truly under the table. But Ralf had also been well established at BMW Williams when I arrived there, so I wasn't particularly worried about being a new boy. It was actually easier settling in with Benetton-Renault when I first arrived than it was with Williams because the people there already knew I could drive a Formula One car, whereas most of the guys at BMW Williams in early 2000 had never heard of me before. There was a big element of risk attached to my arrival there; everyone knew the team had taken a huge gamble.

What Jenson had done already in Formula One was remarkable and I had no doubt that we had signed an outstanding talent. A lot of people were comparing him with Michael Schumacher, and I could see why. We also signed Michael when he was a young driver. But I didn't want to make comparisons, because that isn't what a young driver needs. Jenson is quick and intelligent and shows a lot of maturity for his age. But he needs time, as all young drivers do.

Flavio Briatore, team chief, Benetton-Renault

It soon became clear that the new engine was going to be late, and that, unfortunately, set the tone for the rest of the season because at a stroke it meant we could only test with the B200, which bore no relation to the B201 which had been designed specifically to accept the new engine. To the outside world everything seemed as rosy as it always does at the beginning of a new season, because people are by nature optimistic and winter is the time of year when you can kid yourself that anything is possible. But as Ron Dennis once said, there is no magic in this game. It's all about hard work and commitment. There are no miracles. That's why things tend to be so cyclical. One team will dominate, the way McLaren did in the late 1980s, but another will be working steadily away and eventually it will become dominant, the way Williams did in the early to mid-1990s, before McLaren came back again. Right now we are in another era of Ferrari domination, just as Formula One saw in the mid-1970s. Benetton, of course, had its spell in the lime-light in the mid-1990s, and will have the beam shone on it again, because that's the way the cycle works.

So while the pundits were suggesting all sorts of possibilities for us in 2001, I maintained a far more pragmatic attitude. I knew we were in for a real struggle in the first half of the season, that we wouldn't be able to show our true colours at least until the second half. When the new team line-up was launched to the world's media on Tuesday, 6 February at the Cipriani Hotel in Venice, before everyone sped across the water to see Giancarlo and me unveil the new B201 in St Mark's Square I told anyone who would listen that they shouldn't expect too much of us to begin with. We were so far behind. In terms of gearing up for the future, the end of the 2001 season was destined to be the important time for us. Obviously at the start of the season it would have been nice to get some results, but I knew we simply weren't going to. That didn't mean that Fisi and I wouldn't be trying everything we could, but I wasn't kidding myself. I knew I would have a very different set of colours in my paintbox at the beginning of 2001 from those I'd had at BMW Williams in the second half of 2000.

The season kicked off in Melbourne early in March. Arriving there, it was difficult to know where the past year had gone. It seemed like only the day before that that man had been whisking Dad and me round Albert Park deep in the middle of the night. But now other newcomers were the men in the spotlight. Kimi Raikkonen, my 'stablemate' at David Robertson's management company, and Fernando Alonso were the men under the media's microscope. I was left to get on with things.

As we drove competitively against the full complement of our opposition for the first time, the scale of the mountain we had to climb finally became apparent: I qualified sixteenth, Fisi seventeenth. We were more than three seconds slower than Michael Schumacher on pole in his Ferrari. I was having to take greater risks than I had to qualify third in the BMW Williams at Spa in August 2000 just to try and stay ahead of the European Minardis. But no-one dwelt on that because I was at the wrong end of the grid. The one encouraging thing was that the B201 was significantly better in slow corners because of our lowline engine, but in the power stakes even Minardi's old chain-driven Ford V10s were leaving us. To add to the misery I had engine problems on the Friday and lost the tread of my right rear Michelin tyre, but the cars are so stiff that I was able to drive back to the pits on three wheels and the remains of the tyre's sidewall. Then I had a gearbox problem on Saturday morning, and after the start of the race itself I received a ten-second stop-and-go penalty because my mechanics hadn't left the grid when they should have. That ruined things for me because I'd worked up to eleventh and was enjoying a good scrap at the time with Jos Verstappen. Later, an electrical problem damaged the exhaust and I had to quit after fifty-three laps.

The race did, however, give me an interesting opportunity to compare my first impressions of the Benetton-Renault team with those I'd had at BMW Williams, but it was difficult because now I had a lot more experience so I saw things differently. Benetton-Renault knew what they were doing, and a lot of their working practices were the same. Of course, each team is going to have some different ideas, but the way things worked was not hugely different from any other team I'd raced with, in Formula Three or elsewhere. The car does the same things and you've got to try to do the same things with it, mechanically and aerodynamically.

Malaysia, a fortnight later, was the next race, and this time it was Fisi who qualified sixteenth with me seventeenth. I finished this one, in eleventh place, which was progress, but I lost a chunk of time in the pits (I wasn't the only one) when the monsoon struck suddenly and early, because in the mad scramble to change to wets Fisi managed to arrive just in front of me. At one stage I was fighting with Gastón Mazzacane in the Ferrari-engined Prost, and there was nothing I could do to get by. Then Hakkinen and Verstappen came up to lap us so I backed off and let them through. Mazzacane seemed to be in a world of his own and held them up, so when they finally got through I went with them. It was the most satisfying thing I'd done all year, but it's hard to get excited when you're driving your nuts off and getting nowhere.

Frank and Patrick could see that I was pretty depressed afterwards, and they gave me some words of encouragement, which I really appreciated. They told me to keep my chin up and look to the future. More than most, they knew the underlying strength of Renault's engineering ability, and they were convinced they'd get it right eventually.

I finished tenth in Brazil on April Fool's Day after qualifying twentieth, but while Fisi finished sixth in the rain I had no reason to celebrate. My car felt awful in the wet conditions and I struggled home after an oil circulation problem had lost me time in the pits. Come Imola we were already beginning to focus on survival rather than racing. This time I was twenty-first on the grid and finished twelfth after my refuelling rig misfired the first time I tried to top up.

Our expectations certainly hadn't been high at the start of the season, but now, after four races, we knew the true scale of our problem. But at least Renault had made progress on the reliability of the engine. There were aspects of its unusual layout that led to vibrations, which in turn affected reliability, so initially Renault had to work on solving that – a vital step before Jean-Jacques and his team could start looking for more horsepower. Renault was pioneering, and pioneers often have arrows shot at them. We were certainly going through a discovery phase at that time. I just had to forget that most of the people who'd been praising me to the skies a year earlier had begun to write me off as a one-hit wonder, and keep reminding myself to be patient. But that's easier said than done for a racing driver.

Barcelona at the end of April was the low point of my season, although one promising note was sounded when I was presented with one of the inaugural 'Bernie' gongs, the equivalent to a motor-racing Oscar, at a function at the Circuit de Catalunya. The awards had been decided back in February at the Grand Prix Party at the Royal Albert Hall, billed as a 'Gala Evening of Stars, Cars and Guitars', which had raised £100,000 for the Brain and Spine Foundation. My award was for 'Newcomer of the Year', and I was flattered to be in the company of Michael Schumacher (he picked up his 'Bernie' for becoming world champion), Murray Walker (who received a Lifetime Achievement award) and Formula One's star medic Professor Sid Watkins (honoured for his outstanding contribution to the safety of Formula One).

Unfortunately, that evening didn't set the tone for the rest of my weekend. Once again I qualified only twenty-first (as I would do yet again in Austria two weeks later) after some last-minute set-up changes caused me to miss my final run. And a lack of power-steering made the car very heavy to drive and aggravated my shoulder problem. For the Sunday morning warm-up I tried a quite different set-up and it made the car feel much, much better, but unfortunately that feeling didn't flow into the race. It was quite scary, because both Fisi and I were passed by Alonso in his Minardi on our way to fourteenth and fifteenth places respectively. We were in fact lapped by him.

This was not turning out to be a great time in my career. A few more rumours began to air themselves about my being replaced because of my shoulder, but all I could do was keep my head down and just weather the storm. At the same time our technical director, Mike Gascoyne, was pushing me to get my act together, to push myself even harder. Fair enough. He was simply saying what he thought because he's a fundamentally open guy and if someone asks him a question he'll answer it truthfully, just the way he sees it. But it wasn't as if the same thought hadn't already occurred to me. I knew right from the start that Fisi was a bloody quick little driver, one who is often underrated. Right from the first race I knew I had a battle on my hands with him, but that was hardly a surprise. There aren't any grannies out there in Formula One. Everyone is quick. You're always going to have to be on your mettle. Like I said before, that's the nature of the game. It's a tough little world we live in, and I was pushing myself as hard as I could. What I needed to do was get more out of the car, and that meant finding a way of working to the optimum with my team, and particularly my race engineers.

One of the things people had commented on most at the end of 2000 was how I'd managed to break through with Patrick Head at BMW Williams. He is not renowned for making life a bowl of cherries for drivers who fall below his high standards. People pointed out what had happened with Heinz-Harald Frentzen and Alex Zanardi, neither of whom had gone the full course. But right from the start I'd tried really hard to get on the right side of both Patrick and Frank. I think it helped that I was confident, without being too cocky, and that I was able to show well and get some results quite early on. That's the main thing with them. If you're bringing in the results, that's what they love, because they're out there to win and they want to see that you're the man who can get the job done.

They have this reputation for not mollycoddling their drivers, young or old. Again, people would talk about the fates of Jacques Laffite, Nigel Mansell and Damon Hill. But I thought Frank and Patrick were great! They were really, really cool. Because I was quite inexperienced maybe they were easier on me, but they were really good to me. I had a great year, didn't have any problems at all. I didn't have Patrick shouting, we didn't argue, we never had any major differences of opinion. Things went really smoothly, even when I made a mistake, as I did in Melbourne and at Spa. They didn't get upset. They seemed to understand and to have patience with me, which I greatly appreciated.

Flavio Briatore is different. He likes winners, and he makes no bones about it. I think this is because he has a different background from Frank and Patrick, who are pure-bred racers. They began in the sport because of their love for it. Frank was a rather erratic driver who admits his talents were better suited to team management, Patrick was a designer with Lola, Britain's biggest proprietary racing car manufacturer. Flavio, by contrast, came into Formula One in 1989 because he was appointed by the Benetton family to take over the running of its team. He does not regard himself as a racer, but as a businessman. In a way he was the first of a new breed of team managers. For him, things are more like a balance sheet. He wants to see results. What he has in common with Frank and Patrick is a reputation for not suffering drivers who aren't delivering the goods. Johnny Herbert, Roberto Moreno, Jos Verstappen, J.J. Lehto, Jean Alesi and Alexander Wurz all had short spells at Benetton before leaving.

But at this level of motorsport nobody gets an easy ride. The stakes are simply too high. You are as good as your last race. It didn't matter a damn if I had qualified third at Spa and fifth at Suzuka the previous year if I was only qualifying twenty-first in San Marino, Spain and Austria this time around. Memories, and patience, are extremely short in this game.

Some drivers, given the nature and size of our troubles within the team, would have been kicking and screaming and breaking the furniture. Several observers criticized me at this time for not doing that. But it's not my style. I'd rather have a reasonable discussion with someone and try to see where we can move ahead, rather than shout at people. Obviously I want to win races because that's my goal; I wouldn't be here if it wasn't. It was very, very tough qualifying for those first six races in 2001, especially after what I'd done the previous year. I think if I had been with a team where I knew things couldn't improve, I wouldn't even have bothered. But there was no point getting angry, though I do sometimes when things don't go my way, because I'm a typical Formula One driver. And I admit that I'm a bit more impatient with people now than I used to be, when things aren't right when they should be. It *is* irritating when things aren't perfect, even little things. But I still believe that the rational approach is the way to iron out problems.

Monte Carlo is definitely one of those circuits where it takes time to get up to speed if you're still in the process of setting up your car, and I struggled there too. While Fisi took tenth place on the grid, I was only seventeenth. My car was understeering horribly and I had brake problems too, which you don't want in Monaco. I just didn't feel comfortable with things. The lack of horsepower also made it difficult to balance the handling, and it was still tough without power-steering. I had to laugh when Gerhard Berger observed that somebody should have been beheaded by now for the lack of it, even though that was a bit harsh. The truth was that everyone in the design department was working flat out. Mike Gascoyne had not had very much input to the design of the car because he was not released from his contract with Jordan until late in the 2000 season, so he was trawling through it as best he could, making changes where he saw fit. At the same time Renault Sport was also flat out, and one of the encouraging things at this time was that we usually had new things to try out, no matter how small. Perhaps they improved reliability, or driveability, or gave us just enough of a power increase to allow us to gear the car better. They weren't dramatic changes, but Formula One isn't about big leaps. It's a matter of making enough small but significant changes until they all add up to something special.

I had a steady race on Monte Carlo's streets and moved up as other people fell out, until I was in seventh place by the chequered flag. It was frustrating not to score a point for sixth, but early understeer had changed to oversteer by the end of the race and Jean Alesi was just too far ahead to catch. After the race somebody remarked to Flavio that they thought I'd done a good job to bring my car home seventh. He allegedly told them that I should have come in sixth. Well, like the others, he's entitled to say what he thinks. It's his job to run the team, and in the heat of the moment that can be a difficult thing to do. Of course he's going to get angry at certain times, especially when things haven't gone right. He wants me to do the best job that I can. He has the team's best interests at heart. As far as racing is concerned, we get on, we talk. Off the circuit we don't really converse. Off the circuit I've got my own friends; he's just 100 per cent on the team management side. And anyway, outside racing there's no reason whatsoever for me to be involved with him or to talk to him. That's perfectly normal.

The qualifying session on 9 June for the Canadian GP saw me take up another low spot on the grid, twentieth, and I had to retire early on in the race with an oil leak. But things started changing for the better at the Nürburgring, where I had a different set-up on the car for the Grand Prix of Europe. It was Fisi's set-up, actually. I qualified twentieth without it, and afterwards we had a major head-scratching session, trying to pinpoint why my car understeered so much and Fisi's didn't. We put his set-up on the car and it seemed to work for the race. I finished thirteenth.

We carried on developing that side of things into Magny-Cours, which was a good meeting, especially as we now had power-steering and another engine upgrade, but I messed up qualifying myself there. After the first corner I should have adjusted the differential, but I was concentrating so much on the lap. You can vary the differential electronically on a Formula One car, adjusting how much slip there is to damp out wheelspin. It's actually quite a simple thing to do; I just forgot to do it. I remembered for my third run, then on my final one I realized just as I got to the Adelaide hairpin that I hadn't done it, so I changed it. But you might as well forget the lap when you do that. It was just too late. So that was a disaster, though Fisi and I were still quite close again, in sixteenth and seventeenth places respectively. I was mad with myself.

In the race on 1 July I ran ahead of him for the first eighteen laps, trying to pass cars we should have qualified ahead of, until things went awry during a long first pit stop and I fell behind him. My car then developed a fuel pressure problem, which lost me time as the engine kept cutting out, so I was obliged to stop at the same time as Fisi did, when we refuelled again on the forty-fourth lap. That wasn't ideal and cost me more time as they had to put a fair bit more fuel in to overcome the problem. Later in the race I had a quick spin because I was pushing so hard and had lots of oversteer, and then I flat-spotted a tyre after locking up the wheels for too long under braking, and had to cope with some serious vibration at high speeds as a result. Right near the finish something, probably the engine, seized in the back end of the car and locked the wheels up, so I spun into the gravel.

A lot hung on the British Grand Prix for me, especially after the way things had gone the previous year. We had tested some revised aerodynamic parts in Barcelona just before the race and had our new launch control system for the first time, so I was feeling optimistic. The car was good in practice on the Friday, especially in the slower corners, and that carried over into Saturday morning. But qualifying was a disappointment. I had high-speed understeer on Michelin's harder tyre, and our new aero package didn't quite do the trick. But I was satisfied to outqualify Fisi by a place. The race itself was Magny-Cours all over again. I led Fisi, but after fourteen or fifteen laps the power-steering failed, which made the car very difficult to drive. Then I lost out during my stop because of traffic: two drivers got past me while I was refuelling, one of them Fisi.

When I came back out I got three blue flags after three laps, signalling that the leaders were about to lap me, so I lost even more time obeying them. It was very frustrating, and a fifteenth-place finish did nothing for me.

We were pretty much two thirds of the way through the racing calendar, and things had been every bit as bad as I had expected. But there was light at the end of the tunnel. I didn't realize it as I used the opportunity of a rare visit to Britain to see relatives and friends and catch up, but better times were just around the corner.

THIRTEEN

LIFE SUPPORT

In any walk of life you need people around you to love and trust. When things are tough, you need these people even more.

The world of Formula One is no ordinary walk. It was once memorably described by McLaren chief Ron Dennis as the 'Piranha Club', and that certainly is a pretty good summary. The sums of money that are involved, and the continuous pressure to succeed and to achieve results, generate a maelstrom so powerful that the unwary can be sucked in then spat out just as they are beginning to readjust. To negotiate your way through all this, and to keep your feet on the ground, you really need to have good people around you. I'm lucky. I have a fantastic family, to whom I owe so much, a wonderful girlfriend whom I love very much, great friends whom I met a long time ago, before I stepped into the Formula One spotlight.

My mum, Simone, and my dad, John, are fantastic. Mum is one of my best friends. She always calls me to find out how my racing is going. She's always been supportive, despite all the worries that any mum would have about her little boy doing dangerous things. Her house is littered with cuttings from newspapers and magazines, anything written about me (I worry about her sometimes . . .). On Mother's Day last year I picked her up in the Ferrari and whisked her up to town for lunch at the Ivy. I probably shouldn't admit it, but it was also the first time I had remembered to give her a card. I'm a bit forgetful about things like that.

And without Dad, I probably would never have got into motorsport. He was the one who got me my first kart, and the one who took me to Clay Pigeon when I demanded to have a go at a place where I could really open it up. Throughout those early years he was the one standing out there in the rain while I was on the track having all the fun, he was the one paying for it, he was the one who gave me the space in which to develop and the encouragement when things were rough, who helped me to focus my energies when I decided that Formula One was where I wanted to be. He never laughed at me when I said that, even though I was only a child. He just did everything he could to help set me on the course that brought me to BMW Williams in 2000. There were times when we ran out of money, but he never told me, never made me feel guilty for the expense he was put to or the sacrifices he had to make in his own life. Perhaps the most remarkable thing about him is that he was never a typical karting dad. Sure, he'd get into it if somebody started having a go at me, but he was always quite happy to keep himself in the background, just like he does now.

Of course we get on each other's nerves at times, especially when we were living our *Men Behaving Badly* life together in Bicester before I got into Formula One. That's only natural when you're together so often, but it's great having him there at races. He's a real character, and I'm proud that people like him. He's a good old boy. We try not to talk about racing all the time, but somehow we seem to end up doing just that.

Mum and Dad had a difficult time when I was six. I had some bumps come up on my neck and shoulders and they took me to our local GP, Dr Blacklidge. He checked me over a few times and referred us to a specialist. It wasn't until I was taken to the Royal United Hospital in Bath that Dad and Mum realized it was a cancer clinic. Fortunately I was blissfully unaware of all this, but there was a chemotherapy ward there, all that sort of thing. Kids with cancer sitting around playing with toys.

Simone and I were devastated. Jens went in for his tests and we went outside into the sunshine for absolutely ages. Not saying anything. It really just knocked us flat, it was such an unbelievable thing. After a long wait they said it was some sort of glandular fever. Not a problem, something they could treat. For Simone and me that was one of the highlights of our life. I think that brought me even closer to Jens, as I'm sure other parents will understand.

John Button

Mum and Dad don't get on, but as a family we all accept that. I was coming up for eight when they separated. I think when you're that young and your parents split it's not such a problem because the only thing you say is 'Why?' and you can't really understand the answer anyway. When you get older and you ask why, you hear what they think and understand it a little bit more, but it's probably rougher that way.

I lived with Mum to start with after the split, until she moved away with her new man. Not far, though, probably only twenty minutes away. She obviously wanted me to go and live with them, but she was big enough to let it be my decision. I didn't want to move away from Frome because of school, so I stayed with Dad in his tiny little house. It had one bedroom, I don't remember there being a television, and the fridge had only champagne and cheese in it. Then, when Dad got everything back together again, he met Pippa, who became my stepmum, and we moved to a bigger place.

I would try to see Mum as often as possible, and obviously she wanted me there as much as possible. So I saw both Mum and Dad quite a lot, and for a kid who's had their parents split up I think I did quite well. I don't think I suffered particularly because of the separation, and I always got lots of pressies, which was good! I love everyone in my family and I'm very close to them. I don't think that coming from a broken home has had any negative influence at all on my outlook on family life. When I'm older I want to get married and have kids, definitely. I'm very happy with my girl-friend, Louise. I'm 100 per cent in love and so's she, but nothing like that will happen yet. Mid to late twenties, whenever we feel it's right.

I really like kids. Some people find it difficult to know what to do with them, but I get lots of practice with my nephew and nieces. I have three sisters. Tanya is the eldest; she's thirty-four and a complete nutter. She's just crazy, doesn't care about anything. It's fantastic. She doesn't have any fears. She's got three kids – Karina, sixteen, Kieran, thirteen, and Katriana, five – so she's pretty full-on with brats at the moment. Tanya's divorced, lives with her boyfriend Gary and is very happy, the happiest she has ever been. The kids love Gary, which is great, and unusual. I don't see them enough, but they are all fans of Uncle Jenson. Samantha is thirty-one and a northerner at the moment (she lives in Leeds). She's cool. I think she works in insurance, but I'm not sure. Her boyfriend, Howard, is a top bloke. My youngest sister, Natasha, is twenty-eight and married to Alex, who is a banker. They have a baby daughter called Mollie. I see Samantha most often because she and Howard come down to London more, but over Christmas we all tend to see more of one another. I want to get them all over to Monaco. We are all pretty close, and we speak often on the phone. They're all very protective of me!

The day I met Louise Griffiths was one of the most important of my life. I even remember the date, 4 September 2000, which is quite sad for a bloke. I'd gone to the preview of *Scary Movie* at the Odeon in Leicester Square with my mate Brad Poole. I'd been invited to attend by a company called Hyperactive, whom I later hired to throw my twenty-first birthday (the company, I thought, had quite an apposite name, given the way I was as a kid). As soon as we walked in there I saw this dark-haired girl standing with her friend, and I just thought, 'Jesus Christ, she looks amazing!' Then, when Brad and I walked upstairs to the cinema, she was in front of us again. She looked round at one point, right at us, and I thought, 'Oh my God!' Now Brad is a good-looking bloke, so I thought she must be looking at him. Good old Brad, surfer dude, he's great with the women. And when we sat down this dark-haired girl was still looking. I was getting excited. She was sitting just down from us; I didn't see much of the film. I spent the entire ninety minutes, or however long it was, gazing at her in the dim light.

When we got outside we bumped into her again. She was just about to leave, but I didn't have any snappy lines to chat her up with. I just left. I was always crap at talking to girls. I don't need to be any good now, of course, but I was always quite nervous in that sort of situation. Brad and I went on to the post-film party at Undercrofts, which is about a quarter of an hour's walk from the Odeon, and I thought the girls had gone. Game over. We got to

Undercrofts, and because *Scary Movie* is a piss-take of horror films there was lots of face-painting going on, people getting scars and stuff. We walked upstairs, and this girl was just standing there. I was half hammered at the time, and still couldn't screw up the courage to talk to her.

A couple of hours went by, then early in the morning she had to leave. She was just about to walk out when Brad hissed at me, 'She's leaving, she's leaving!' So I ran outside before it was too late. I found this bloke actually trying to touch her up on her way out, so obviously I went over and sorted him out. 'Oh, thank you, you're amazing!' the girl said to me. I asked her why she was leaving so soon, and she replied, 'Well, you've had all night to talk to me.' Then she stole my phone out of my back pocket and put her number in it. She gave me a peck on the cheek and that was it. She left. I went back upstairs and enjoyed the rest of that night very much!

It took a week of phone calls to finally persuade her to go out with me, but it was worth it. I think Louise had reservations about going out with a racing driver. Our reputations must precede us. But I think she's just fantastic. We laugh at the same things and finish each other's sentences. She's very calm and gives me a lot of support. When they first met Louise, my family didn't know what to think because she's very attractive. But when they got to know her, it was, wow! When you really get to know her, her personality is fantastic too. A lot of women are good-looking, but Louise is something else.

Soon after we started going out I decided to look at a flat in Monaco, and I asked her if she wanted to come along. I thought it was a pretty cool line. In fact, I couldn't think of anything better than that. I was testing in Monza at the time, and I asked her what she was doing over the next couple of days. She said she was doing nothing, so I asked her if she wanted to come to Monte Carlo and look at some places. But then she said, nice and calmly, 'Oh no, sorry. I think I might have to work, actually.' I knew she was bull-shitting, but it was a good enough reason. She didn't want to be taken in by all the glamour. She wanted to meet me just like a normal person, which was good. I respected her for that.

Louise follows my racing really closely. She gets a bit worried when she's at home and I'm away at races, but she came to a few of the meets in 2001 and she was a lot happier. She cares a lot about what I do and she understands if I'm in a bad mood on the telephone, which I was quite often during my first season with Benetton. She and Dad bore the brunt of the stressful times I was having, but Louise is 100 per cent understanding, which is great for me. I wish she could be with me more often, but she has her own life to lead and her own career to sort out. She's a singer and songwriter with a girl band. What's good is that with her music she has a lifestyle similar to mine. If I had a girlfriend with a nine-to-five job, or with no job at all, just sitting at home waiting for me to arrive, that wouldn't be any good for either of us. It's interesting for me as well, to see what she's doing. Like me, she's spending a lot of her time on something she has a passion for. Hopefully, when the band is launched she'll be able to come to more races.

After Monaco in 2001 it was a mutual decision between the team and myself that it would be good if I had space on my own at the races just to think about the drive 100 per cent. That went for my managers, too. It's true that you worry about people, get caught up in what they want to do in the evening, making sure they aren't bored, which is inevitably a distraction. Lou wasn't able to come to the last few races of the 2001 season anyway because her record company wanted to shape any publicity she got. And I'm sure it's going to get more difficult to meet up because she'll be very busy in 2002. But, I repeat: I think it's great that she's got something like that. It's exciting for me as well. I really want to see her career take off.

Louise and my family are my anchors. Monaco is my home, and Louise is there as often as she can be. When she isn't there, I'll fly my family over. My previous long-term relationship, with Kimberley Keay, was nothing like as solid. It ended on a sour note.

I'd gone out on and off with Kim ever since we first met in 1996, when I was still karting and before I won the European Formula A Championship, but we never actually lived together. People, though, will say we were childhood sweethearts, I suppose! Racing didn't really put a strain on our relationship; sometimes people split up because things just aren't right between them. In the end, that was the case with us. It had nothing to do with my becoming a Formula One driver and wanting to trade up to a new model, or anything as crass as that, because I don't think I've changed an awful lot as a person despite the way things in my life have been transformed so dramatically. I think Kim felt a little sore afterwards, that maybe the break-up was to do with the racing. I think she had a hard time being stuck in Frome while I travelled the world and saw great things. Her feelings must still have been sore when she sold her story to a tabloid newspaper. But I don't bear her any ill will. We had some good times together, and these things happen.

Fame is a funny thing, but I believe I know 100 per cent who my friends are. It's important to me to keep my old mates. I always tried to see them as often as I could when I was racing karts in Europe or driving in Formula Ford or Formula Three. There'd be a house party or whatever and we'd get together, or I'd see them when I went down to Somerset to visit my family. We'd go surfing in Croyde and spend a lot of time together. They are pretty special still, and I try to see them as much as possible. The only way to do that now when the season is on is for them to come to Monaco. When they came over last year I offered to pay for their flights because they should all have been studying at uni, but none of them let me. And when we were there all of them insisted on paying their way. I might pay for something, but they'd say, 'OK, we'll pay for the next one.' All week it was like that. It was really good of them. Just like being back at school, except that we were in the south of France on a 72ft boat, living it up.

I read somewhere recently that Fay Tozer of Steps said that the thing about fame was that it changed the way people saw you, even if it didn't change the way you saw yourself. I know what she means. Sometimes it puts distance between you and other people, as if there's an invisible aura around you that keeps them away. I'm not rude if I'm out in London, for example, and people want to come and talk to me, but I'll make it short and sweet and then I'm off. I think I'm a pretty open, sociable sort of bloke, although when I first meet someone it can be difficult to know whether to trust them or not. I don't really have a set of criteria I use to check them out, or anything like that. To tell the truth, I'm much more interested in whether or not they're friendly and come across as sincere. After all, 98 per cent of what we say is bullshit. Social bullshit. Then again, you can meet people who are overly friendly and you know they're doing that for one reason: they think you're different to them. I just like people to be themselves. It's always a good start.

I don't really trust new people straight off, although obviously I wait to see and make compensations here and there just like anybody else. If it's a journalist, I start to trust them only when I see that they're paying attention to what I'm actually saying, rather than just writing what they think. Sometimes there really isn't any point in doing an interview, there really isn't. I suppose that by nature I'm just not a trusting person. There really aren't many people I trust, especially in Formula One. Jackie Stewart once said that he didn't trust anyone. He didn't mean it nastily, he was just being practical. I trust my family and Louise completely and I trust my closest friends, those I've had since I was very young, but there aren't many people apart from them in whom I feel I could confide. There are a few, but not many.

Two people who have been very important in my life outside my family and friends are my former managers, David Robertson and Harald Huysman. In July 1998 I was invited to go and have a chat about my future with Ron Dennis at McLaren. It was a kind gesture from one of the big guns of the sport, the sort of meeting any young driver covets. I went with David and Harald. There was a brief introductory chat with Ron, then he politely suggested that David and Harald go downstairs and wait in reception so that he could speak with me alone.

Ron's first words to me when David and Harald had left the room were that I should get rid of them because they were feeding off my career. As if I was just a dumb, naive kid who didn't know how many beans make four. He then offered to bankroll my career from Formula Ford through to whatever he felt I was suited to. That might have been Formula One with McLaren, but it might also have meant sportscars with Mercedes-Benz or DTM touring car racing with the Stuttgart manufacturer. At that time Ron had several drivers, such as Nick Heidfeld, Ricardo Zonta and Dario Franchitti, under similar contracts.

In its own way it was a great offer; it was meant well and meant sincerely. But there was no way I was going to dump two people who had helped my career. Some people might have been tempted, but that's just not my style. I place a high value on loyalty.

Harald based himself in Belgium during his days in the 1980s and 1990s as a racing driver in Formula Ford and Formula Three. He's a charming and very enthusiastic guy and I'm sure he won't take offence if I say that his car control didn't always match up to his undoubted speed. In 1985 he had a lot of shunts while racing in Formula Three for Eddie Jordan's team. But because he went through the mill Harald not only came to understand precisely how the motor-racing world works, but also who makes it work. I thought that Eddie knew everyone who was anyone, but Harald runs him mighty close.

Harald stopped racing at the end of 1994 and started various businesses, including car dealerships and an indoor kart track and racing school in Norway. He was one of the first people in car racing to believe in my ability, and for that I will always be grateful.

Without people such as all of these and my closest friends behind me, I would have struggled, for sure.

FOURTEEN

TURNING THE CORNER

When you get into the sort of downward spiral in which I found myself at the beginning of the 2001 season, you take whatever comfort you can get. I had mentally written off the year as far as the sort of results I had enjoyed the previous year were concerned. I had accepted that the transition period Benetton was undergoing as it prepared to metamorphose into Renault for 2002 would have to take precedence over the development of my career, even though I was still learning a huge amount as a driver. But other people didn't see it that way. I came in for a fair amount of criticism on a number of fronts in those early months, criticism that concentrated on my professional and private lives. So I was chuffed when our chief engineer, Pat Symonds, stepped in to put things into a sensible perspective for the media.

The difference between Jenson and Giancarlo was quite small. People underestimate the value of continuity. Giancarlo had been with the team for a fair few years, so

we knew what he thought and what he liked. Jenson was new to the team. There is no doubt that he is a very, very rapid driver and that he could do better than we were allowing him to at that stage. It was really down to continuity and very little else.

Pat Symonds, Chief Engineer, Benetton-Renault

As I got my head down and worked for my new team, I was naturally keeping a close eye on the performance of BMW Williams in general and Ralf Schumacher and Juan Pablo Montoya in particular. You didn't need to be a genius to figure out that with three of us under contract and only two race seats available, somebody was going to be disappointed sooner or later when the musical chairs game finally stopped. Ralf had won his first Grand Prix at Imola on 15 April, and towards the end of May Frank and Patrick re-signed him for another two years. His contract had been due to expire at the end of 2002, when my current contract with Renault expires and when Juan Pablo's contract is also up. Now that Ralf was staying until the end of 2004, it put Juan Pablo and me under even greater pressure: him to retain the seat, me to regain it. This naturally placed me at a disadvantage. Montoya had the perfect equipment with which to showcase his considerable talent; I was still struggling as we worked to make our car more competitive.

We signed up Ralf for 2003 and 2004 and that takes us to the end of our current contract with BMW, as it exists now. For 2002 we will have Juan Pablo Montoya in the other car, but I imagine part of the way through 2002 we will have to make a decision about what we will do for 2003 and maybe 2004. It's certainly not something that I anguish over at the moment, and I don't think Frank

does, either. Obviously we were concerned that Jenson looked to be having a difficult time at Benetton-Renault. But we were impressed with him enough times over the year he was with us to think that he is very talented and I can only imagine that there was some limitation in his car. It was difficult to imagine that they would have been giving Giancarlo better equipment. I think that Fisichella is very quick and I suspect that the car was maybe a bit difficult to drive, and Fisichella, with his four or five years of experience, was handling that problem better than Jenson was. But I wasn't going to be surprised if Jenson came back before the end of the year because he is an intelligent guy, he's not a child. He realizes it's a tough game and he wasn't going to be looking inwardly and thinking, 'This isn't fair.' He was working out how he was going to come back. So when he did begin coming back strongly in the latter part of the year, it wasn't a surprise.

Patrick Head, Technical Director, Williams F1 team

There's a misguided assumption that all a Formula One driver needs to do to go faster is to push harder. It's a bit like that old clichéd scene in motor-racing movies when the hero is fighting for the race and suddenly you see him push harder on the throttle. Well, real life isn't like that. In Formula One everyone is already flat out – that's why it's so tough. I knew perfectly well that the answer to my problems at Benetton lay not in any greater physical effort, because I was already doing plenty of that. Instead, I had to be patient and use my head. I had to work through the problems with my engineers. Between us we had to devise a better method of working together, of setting up the car so that I could be as con-fident in it as Giancarlo was in his. That was going to take time, but while we were working through that process we could also take advantage of the many changes the technical department was bringing on line.

Slowly, things got better. I think of Hockenheim at the end of July as the turning point of our season, and not just because it's where I scored my first points for Benetton. Within the team, my race engineer Rod Nelson and my electronics man Paul Monaghan had swapped places, and suddenly our relationships were all freshened up. Everything clicked, and we all began working really well together. At Monza the week before we'd had our first really good test of the season. For the first time the team was able to run two of the B201 cars as opposed to one B201 and one of last year's Supertec-engined B200s. Giancarlo and I covered more mileage in that test than in any other we'd done all season. It was a really productive time that helped significantly when we got to Germany. Pat Symonds calculated that up until that point we'd done about 30 per cent of the testing the team had done the previous season, which shows you where a lot of our problems lay. We just hadn't been able to put in the mileage, and in Formula One the more you test the faster you go.

The B201 felt very good. It had always been reasonably good under braking, which is very important on a track where you can reach 350kph on the straights and then have to brake to around 100kph to get through each of the three chicanes and then into the stadium section at the end of the lap. We were helped here too because the Michelin tyres had a definite advantage over the Bridgestones in the high ambient temperature, and the extra grip under braking was particularly useful. But I never thought Hockenheim would give us our best chance because of the engines. The circuit places a massive premium on engine power and reliability because you spend so much time at full revs in top gear.

The car wasn't too bad in the first two Friday sessions, when I was running a different tyre to Fisi, and in the end it felt quite a lot better, once I'd dialled out the oversteer which was making the back end of the car step out in corners. We were running reasonably similar set-ups by then, and I was a lot happier. We were both quick, Fisi eleventh and me fifteenth. For the first time that season we looked pretty good in comparison to a lot of the cars out there. On such a quick track it made a lot of people sit up and take notice, because they all thought we were way down on power. It showed how much progress we had quietly been making.

My fears about reliability seemed to have foundation when I had a gearbox problem on the Saturday morning, then my engine blew up on my final run in qualifying. That was really disappointing because I was on my way to outqualifying Giancarlo, who's always very quick in Germany. I qualified only eighteenth after all that, a place behind Giancarlo, but we knew that neither position was a true reflection of our improved status.

I got a good start in the race and by the end of the first lap I had climbed to thirteenth, two places ahead of Fisi and not far behind the two Jordans, Jacques Villeneuve, and Jos Verstappen in his Arrows. By the time I stopped to refuel on the twenty-fourth lap I was up to seventh, and we had a clear chance of points. Unfortunately, stopping sooner rather than later wasn't the way to go, and on his worn tyres Fisi was able to leapfrog me by the time he stopped two laps later. After he got out of the pits ahead of me and then survived a brief off-track moment, we circulated together, running at the same speed all the way to fourth and fifth places.

The relief for the team was enormous. We hadn't just lucked in because a lot of other people fell out, we were genuine points contenders. My car was well balanced all day and we were faster than the Jordans and the BARs while running the same fuel loads. The only problem I had all afternoon was when I inadvertently pulled my drinks bottle tube out of my mouth so that I got sprayed in the face every time I braked. In the circumstances, I could live with that. The two points finishes were precisely the sort of fillip we'd been looking for all season, a sign that we were really beginning to make progress. Everyone else was stunned, not only by our speed but by our reliability on a track that traditionally breaks cars. For sure, getting power-steering helped us a lot, but so did all the little upgrades and aerodynamic changes Benetton and Renault had been producing for the cars.

Personally, I saw Hockenheim as further confirmation that I'd got on par with Fisi and was fitting in at Benetton-Renault. It certainly helped me when I started setting my car up in a similar fashion to Fisi. We have different driving styles, so initially we didn't think there would be much benefit in using the same set-up. I was having to find my way early on, and he already knew what he liked and so did his engineers. That counts for quite a lot when you have only two hours' running on Friday and an hour and a half on Saturday prior to qualifying, especially when the amount of testing you can do is limited, and given that I frequently had mechanical problems in practice and didn't always get out to run the car during a race-morning warm-up because Renault wanted to conserve its engines for the race.

Formula One cars are very complicated machines. There is so much that you can adjust mechanically and aerodynamically, and then there are all the electronics too. You can adjust all the angles of the suspension: camber, toe-in, toe-out, castor. You can adjust the ride height, which controls the car's ground clearance and has a massive influence on the amount of downforce it generates. You can adjust the weight distribution by moving the ballast around – we do that a lot for qualifying. Then you can change the type of wings you run: at the rear you might try a biplane with only two main upper elements to go with the lower element, or a triplane with three upper elements; you can change the angles at which they run; you can add Gurney flaps to the trailing edges to generate more downforce. You can also adjust how much assistance there is in the power-steering; how much slip you have in the differential; how much help you want from the traction control. The permutations are almost endless. And that's standard, without factoring in any little thoughts the engine people might come up with.

It's all massively complex, which is why you need a lot of running time to enable you not only to understand the car fully, but to get to know which set-ups work for you and which don't – and you don't get good running time if the car's unreliable in the first place. Obviously, the best car is one with neutral handling. That means that the front and rear ends work in harmony, with equal amounts of grip. The car will behave itself nicely in corners and will just track through them as if it's on rails. If I can't have that I'd rather have a little bit of understeer, where the front end doesn't always want to follow the line you choose with the steering wheel, than oversteer, where the back end is always stepping out of line. Understeer can be time-consuming and frustrating, but it's better than oversteer, which can make the car spin. That loses you a lot more time.

It's essential that you work very closely with your engineers. It's a bit like a marriage: gradually each side gets to know what the other likes and how to go about achieving it; sometimes you fall out over things, but most of all you have to keep working at it. To begin with, I just couldn't find the way to go. The main problem was braking. We couldn't run the car as low at the front as Fisi did. I brake harder than he does; my initial hit on the pedal is harder than his. Because of that I would lock my front wheels if I ran the same front ride height as Fisi. But of course, the lower you run the car the better it helps with the downforce because the whole floor area of the car functions better. I tend to brake earlier, think about the corner, find the apex and then run through it. I got some flak from the engineers early on because I think they thought it was a bit cissy to brake early. It's the macho thing, isn't it, braking super-late? But Alain Prost used to brake early and it didn't do him any harm, because he got on the gas quicker. I think my style is similar to his. What braking early can do, however, is upset the aerodynamics on some circuits, so it took me a while to find a good set-up and a good compromise on style to get the best out of the car.

Eventually we found a way with the set-up, I changed my style very slightly and Rod and Paul swapped jobs, and the combination of those three things really helped a lot. We began to figure these things out at the Nürburgring at the end of June, but circumstances would prevent me proving their worth once and for all until the last few races of the season.

At the high-downforce Hungaroring in mid-August we had a new spoon-shaped front wing and a few other little things that didn't seem to make much difference there, though since then they've worked really well. The new wing made the car less pitch sensitive and therefore a lot more driveable, which was a big step forward. It calmed the car down under braking, for instance, which was a good thing. The car used to be very twitchy before when you braked hard. I qualified seventeenth – I had to use the spare car after my race car broke its engine in the morning – Fisi fifteenth. The spare car had quite a few things on it that Fisi liked and I didn't, among them different steering arms that made the car feel much heavier. It just didn't suit my style.

On race day I got a stop and go for jumping the start, and that killed things for me there and then. I was running way down at thirty-four laps when I got a bit sideways coming out of the last corner and got too out of shape for the traction control to stop me spinning and stalling.

I went to Spa, a favourite track of mine, really looking forward to getting back up towards my 2000 performance level, especially as the car had been flying during testing the previous week in Barcelona. I really felt that we were on the right track, but again I was destined to be disappointed. We had one of those disjointed weekends Spa's changeable weather can throw at you.

On the Friday Fisi was fourth and I was tenth after the engine had to be changed after the morning's session and I got just the one run in the dry. When it began to rain and I switched to wets I made a mistake at the Bus Stop and broke a track-rod after clipping the wall. I didn't realize it, but that was to prove an accurate dress rehearsal for my race. Qualifying itself was an absolute lottery. It was wet for most of the session with a narrow window at the end when those who got out on dry tyres really made big improvements. Fisi was one of them, and he qualified eighth; I wasn't, and finished fifteenth. I'd gone for intermediates instead, which was a mistake.

The 2001 Belgian Grand Prix was another race with a restart, after Luciano Burti and Eddie Irvine tangled four laps in. Luciano's was a big shunt: he went head-on into the tyres at Blanchimont, which is the fastest corner on any European circuit. We take it in top gear at over 300kph. Fortunately my old Formula Three sparring partner escaped from a very ugly accident with nothing worse than some unpleasant bruising, but for a while a lot of people were fearing the worst. At the restart I got away brilliantly and was ahead of the McLarens going into La Source, which meant that Fisi was second and I was about fourth. But unfortunately the front end didn't have the grip to maintain my speed through the hairpin and I got outgunned on the run to Eau Rouge.

The most annoying aspect of my tricky weekend was that I never did more than a lap during the race-morning warm-up. That meant that I had no chance to scrub in my new tyres for the race, so I went into it knowing that I would have to do that during the early laps. That's no way to go racing. At that point of the season the new Michelins really needed to be nursed for about fifteen laps to stabilize them, otherwise the rubber simply began graining, or rolling across the tread, which would kill the grip level. Fisi had nicely scrubbed tyres, I didn't. While I was waiting for them to come in, the world and his wife went blasting by. Fisi was running up there in second place, fending off David Coulthard's McLaren for all he was worth, and I was trailing round like some sort of chump without the same opportunity to shine. I was seriously unhappy. And I was even unhappier when the tyres set the car sliding as I turned into the Bus Stop. I just clipped the plastic marker in the right-hand flick, and that was enough to tear off my front wing. Without any downforce, I slid into the outer wall. I looked a complete idiot. I tried to forget that as I watched Fisi go on to take the flag in third place – Benetton's only podium finish of the season. He is very quick round Spa anyway, but obviously the car had to be pretty good to do what it did there. It wasn't as quick as the Ferraris or the McLarens, but Coulthard couldn't overtake him for a long time and that augured well for the remaining races.

I went off to Monza in the second week of September even more determined to show everyone what I could do with a car that worked properly. Eleventh fastest after a good qualifying session endorsed the progress we were making. I'd had one of the best Fridays of my season, and it was good to see that form carry on through to Saturday afternoon. The car felt really good, and I felt I'd proved a point. Especially as I outqualified Fisi.

The Italian Grand Prix fell just five days after the terrorist attacks on the World Trade Center in New York, so everyone was still in a bit of a daze after lifting their heads earlier that week from the insular business of Formula One long enough to look at the outside world. I don't know anyone in the paddock who wasn't touched in some way by those atrocities. Then Alex Zanardi had a horrible accident during a ChampCar race at the Lausitzring in Germany on the Saturday afternoon. Word in the paddock initially suggested that he had been killed, then we learned that he had had to have both legs amputated. The two things combined to lend an unpleasant, brooding atmosphere to what is normally one of the most fizzing paddocks on the Formula One calendar.

Come race day, the mood was still sombre. Michael Schumacher, who had clearly been deeply upset by events, was talking about not racing in two weeks' time at Indianapolis. As we began our parade round the circuit on the back of a big flatbed truck, he began to solicit support for a no-overtaking pact through the first two chicanes of the opening lap. He ended up having a blazing row with Villeneuve, who refused point blank. As the argument dragged on in the paddock, the FIA said that it would leave the decision up to the drivers. If they were unanimous, then they would consider allowing a single-file start. But as long as Jacques was going to stand firm it all became academic, even though Michael continued to try to enlist support on the grid. As far as Giancarlo and I were concerned, the matter was taken completely out of our hands. Flavio told us that we were going to race, so that was that. No single file for us.

It was a really difficult situation for the drivers, over and above the fact that it was a difficult weekend for everyone after what had happened earlier in the week, and then Alex's accident. But some thought Michael's fears also went back to the accident the previous year at Monza as a result of which a marshal had been killed. If that was the case, some argued, the time to have made representations was months ago, not now on race morning. Villeneuve got all the attention and any flak that was going because of the stand he made, but I admired him for having the courage of his convictions. No-one wants to look like the bad boy, but there were a few other drivers who wanted to race, and that's what we were there to do after all. That's what the spectators were paying for, and the start is often the most exciting thing to watch in a race. They had paid good money to see something.

Back in 1970, when Jochen Rindt was killed in practice, Jackie Stewart still raced even though Jochen had been his best friend. There was nothing callous about it. Even in the face of tragedy you have to carry on. What was the use of us not racing? Why did we qualify? Why did we do anything that weekend? If all the other drivers had agreed to line up in single file to go through the first corner, I would have found it difficult to object because I would have felt terrible going against a united front, but that's just me. I certainly wouldn't have done what I subsequently did, move out off the start line and fly down the inside, if the agreement *had* been to go single file, because that wouldn't have been playing the game. But ultimately the decision was taken to race as usual.

I made a fantastic start, leaping up to sixth place from eleventh as we headed to the first corner. What happened next, I admit, was fully my fault. It happens to most of us from time to time; you just misjudge things slightly. I got a lot of stick from some of my fellow drivers for it, which I can understand. But I thought it a bit much when some righteously pretended that they had been circumspect going into the chicane. I don't know if anyone was trying to be careful, whatever that might mean in such circumstances. I don't care what they say anyway; for the race everyone was at 100 per cent. Nobody was reining in. The two Ferraris locked up into the first corner. You don't do that if you're going gently. I got shit-canned for trying to go down the inside and hitting Trulli when the line proved too slippery to stop in time, but Frentzen confirmed that the outside line was really slippery. I'm told that Michael passed Ralf in between the two Lesmo corners with his two right-hand wheels on the grass. After all that he'd said and done that morning!

It was a difficult one. If you're doing something artificial it's always dangerous. A driver's inclination is to race; if you try to race without really racing, at say 80 or 90 per cent, you're bound to have a situation where incidents occur. It's bad enough when everyone's following their natural instincts.

On the run to the first corner I saw Button in my mirrors speeding too fast on the inside after the start. Benetton was clearly desperate to get some points, but that clearly didn't do Jenson any good. It was always going to end in tears. The ridiculous thing is that even when you warn people, they still think they can brake ten metres later than they do in qualifying. He went far too fast into the first chicane – I could see him – and I just think he was wrong to do so.

David Coulthard, Formula One driver, McLaren

I know DC gave me a bit of a mauling in the press afterwards. Obviously I hear about these things, and I read some things. I think in *Autosport* he said I was over-ambitious or something like that. But it was a racing incident. How many other people crashed at the start of a race in 2001? I was sorry for what I did, but I didn't think it was any more over-ambitious than anyone else's efforts over the year that had a similar outcome.

Unfortunately, when I arrived too fast at the chicane and collected Trulli's Jordan I took my front wing off. Trulli spun into retirement, and I had to drive slowly round to the pits for a new nose. Just as I was starting out again to catch the tail-enders and get settled into a recovery, the engine blew up. So, all in all, it was a very disappointing weekend, because I think the car would have been very quick in the race.

A few more little tweaks on the aerodynamic side (it's amazing how much you can gain just by running a different wing on the car) and another step up on the engine side from Renault went hand in hand with our preparations for the US Grand Prix at Indianapolis on 30 September. We certainly weren't up there with the BMW, the Ferrari or McLaren's Mercedes engine in terms of sheer power, but things were looking a lot better and it was still only the first year with a brand new and quite radical engine. I'm not pretending that we were cock-a-hoop while we were struggling so much in the early days, but it had become a source of great satisfaction to see how much the engine was improving with every race.

At Indianapolis the car again worked well. Even more importantly, the tyres worked well too. They were good not just on lap times but in terms of consistency over a number of laps. Although the rears still had a tendency to grain slightly, I had found in testing a week before Indy that the situation wasn't as bad as it sounded. Instead of having to drive round and round quite carefully for fifteen or more laps just to get the tyres past the graining stage, we could pretty much go straight out and start doing the real testing we were there to do.

Having Michelin in Formula One has been a definite bonus. Our policy in testing was always to spend time working with the tyre and getting it to suit our car, and vice versa, and while that takes up a lot of time it's also important to know the different specification tyres' individual characteristics. There was never any point in just accepting from Michelin the feedback from other Michelin users. It was important that we took the time to gather our own specific data, not just for this year's car but for next year's. Michelin was also listening more to what we had to say because we were getting closer to the front. They listened in the first half of the year too, of course, but they didn't take a lot of data from our cars because we were so far back then. Now we had more to offer.

And there was another benefit to the tyre war. In the overall package of engine, chassis, tyres and driver, the tyres can contribute the greatest chunk of time. A different type of compound, for example, can win you a second a lap. To gain the equivalent jump with an engine you'd have to find another 100bhp, maybe more, when the usual increment in terms of development is between 5bhp and 10bhp.

I was pleasantly surprised by how competitive we were in practice on the Friday morning in Indianapolis. Things had clicked between me and my engineers, we understood each other better, so now we could go out in practice and be quick straight away. I ended the day thirteenth, even though I'd used new tyres early on and it transpired that the later you put them on the faster you went. So I knew I had a good chance of qualifying well. I like the Indy track, so it was a fun day. There hadn't been too many of them recently.

On Saturday I managed, after dialling out some alarming initial understeer, to produce the best qualifying result of my season to that point when I took tenth on the grid, and I was really happy with that. Mike Gascoyne was happy too! I was third fastest through the speed trap as well, which was good news. I'd been slip-streaming Rubens Barrichello's Ferrari at the time, but even so the car was good in a straight line and we were running less wing than most. We'd need that in the race, too, if we were going to have a chance of overtaking anyone into the first corner. Slipstreaming is very important at Indy. I did my best lap while I was behind Barrichello, but unfortunately a subsequent attempt to get a tow from Ralf didn't work out quite so well. Some teams actually sent both drivers out to tow each other round. We thought about that tactic during the week, but it's a difficult thing to organize with all the other traffic, and it means that one driver has to sacrifice a run to let the other one get the quick lap, so we thought it was better just to wait for a chance behind other cars. Let them do the work for us.

It was quite funny, actually. It reminded me of my old Formula Ford days when people would wait for me to tow them round on a quick lap. At Indy you'd see all these cars out on the circuit slow-ing down when they saw somebody coming up behind them so they could then follow them and try to get a tow. Everyone wanted to let everyone else go by, but of course nobody wanted to be the one to overtake and give someone else a ride. Good fun. It made qualifying a lot more exciting. It was the best Saturday I had all year. If I hadn't made a bit of a mistake on my last attempt while I was trying to slipstream Ralf, I think my time would have been really promising.

Yet again I was reminded that one of the most gratifying aspects of racing at Indianapolis is the support from the American public. There weren't as many spectators as there had been for the first race the previous year, but there were still a lot of people at the

Brickyard and they were all determined to make the event a success. You simply couldn't have hoped to count how many American flags there were, and the atmosphere was one of tremendous solidarity and nationalism, especially during the singing of the national anthem on race-day morning. A lot of the screaming in the stands opposite the pits was for Juan Pablo Montoya, naturally, but the whole thing was fantastic. It was a really good buzz, especially after Monza. They certainly know how to put on an event at Indianapolis.

I really wanted to finish the year with a good result, and this was my second last chance to do just that. Somebody pointed out that a really stunning result could turn everything around for me in terms of how some people perceived me, but I don't really think like that to be honest. I was just focused on doing the very best I could with the machinery at my disposal. I finished ninth eventually, close behind Fisi, after Jarno Trulli had frustrated my start by chopping across my bows heading to the first corner. It was all kosher stuff, but I'd hoped for better after the starts we'd been making. I also made a boob during my pit stop. The rear brakes had been locking up so I'd wound the brake bias to the front, but when I made my stop I forgot I'd done it and lost time after locking up the front wheels and sliding beyond the refuelling rig.

My final chance for points in 2001 came in October at Suzuka, a circuit I love. As usual I found my way round reasonably cautiously as far as braking and turning and accelerating were concerned, then picked up the rhythm. I was delighted that the Benetton-Renault was better there than it had been any-where else all season, although I had a lot of understeer on the Friday morning. We changed the car but went too far, so it got a bit oversteery, but on new tyres the balance was a lot better.

Unfortunately, the engine began to lose power after a couple of laps and then died on the straight. The team diagnosed a fuel leak problem.

We had another new engine for qualifying. All the way through the rev range it seemed good. You can never actually feel a 10bhp increment, but it showed up as being better on the telemetry and made a difference on the lap times. At the same time, however, I was losing huge amounts of time in the esses, with understeer. I just didn't set my car up as well as Fisi did, and I lost all my time to him there. I was faster than him in the second sector and through the last one we were equal; the four-tenths difference between our times was all down to the esses, where I'd been so quick the previous year. I had the fourth slowest time. Every time we tried to change things, it made either the car twitchy or no difference at all. Eventually we began to suspect that the car's handling was very sensitive to the traction control setting being used at any given moment.

Sixth and ninth on the grid, though, was enormously encouraging for the team. Fisi did a good job. I didn't think he'd be that quick; I thought we'd be closer. But that understeer in the early section made a huge difference, and he'd obviously got his car sorted a little bit better through there than I had. You never really know where you're going to be in qualifying these days, but what I did know was that the car was just getting better and better. Eleventh in qualifying at Monza, tenth at Indianapolis, ninth in Suzuka. I was telling people that I'd be on pole for the British Grand Prix in 2002. All the new bits the team and Renault had been producing endlessly were paying off.

We had a great chance of scoring some points, and an opportunity to secure seventh place in the Constructors' Championship.

As it turned out, that's precisely where Benetton finished. In the race only the top three teams beat me (Fisi had had to retire), which was really satisfying, though it would have been nice to have gained another place and taken a point.

We gave Giancarlo a send-off party afterwards, before I headed back to the UK to visit my family and friends. I hadn't known what to expect of him when I joined Benetton, but I know now that he's very quick and he gets on it. It was always hard running against him, which is the way it should be, but from Magny-Cours onwards we were a lot closer. He was a good team-mate, and a good bloke. We got on.

It's hard to compare him with Ralf – something a lot of people ask me to do – because they're different drivers and they're in different cars. Maybe Fisi suited the Benetton better than I did, and maybe last year I sometimes suited the Williams better than Ralf did. But Ralf is quick too.

So that was the end of my second season in Formula One. It was an interesting time for me, for sure, because it was the first time in my career that I'd come up against really negative comments about what I was doing, some of it really harsh criticism. There'd been a bit of that in 2000, but generally it was all quite good. I understand that there's always going to be negative publicity for somebody in the pit lane; in 2001, I guess it was my turn. People have to write something, after all. But, yeah, it was an experience. It was easy for some of the people who were upset by the wave of hype I'd found myself riding the previous year to turn round and say, 'See? I told you so.' You'll always find people who are that smart, whatever line of work you're in. But drawing fire like that is one of the downsides of actually getting out and doing something rather than just sitting on your backside at home watching television or whatever. I wasn't really surprised by it. When you're quick, people don't like it; when you're slow, they're really going to be down on you. But it's not a problem. I just learned to put up with it. And I had plenty of practice in 2001.

FIFTEEN

A SENSE OF PERSPECTIVE

I've learned two things as a result of living my life in the public gaze: one is that people will think what they want about you, regardless of whether or not it is accurate; the other is that at all times you need to keep a sense of perspective.

A lot of people thought Flavio gave me a massive bollocking after Monaco because I had my boat *Little Missy* moored right there by the harbour and Louise was there with some of her friends from the pop group Atomic Kitten. But that wasn't true. Flavio didn't have a problem with any of that, and there was no reason for him to say anything about my public image because I never went out. That's what I didn't understand about all the grief the media gave me for 'high living' around that time. It wasn't the best place in the paddock for the boat, perhaps, but I didn't choose it. I just got what I was given by the harbour master. I would far rather have been tucked away, not in such a high-profile position, but maybe he thought he was doing me a favour.

I heard what people were muttering about Jenson and the possessions he has acquired, but I saw nothing wrong in that. He's young and enjoying himself. It was perfectly natural. What I did see – and perhaps others did not – was a dedicated, talented young driver who was experiencing many problems and taking them in his stride without creating any fuss. We had not yet been able to give him a competitive car after introducing a revolutionary new engine and there had been many teething problems. He tolerated our shortcomings. He was very patient, very calm, very English! But I wanted to see him get upset and angry. I thought he should lose his temper with us, but in a positive way, and start making more demands.

Years ago, when Michael Schumacher was with us and we were creating the team that won two world titles, he had that anger. He was very severe with himself and with the team as well. It would be unfair to compare Jenson with Michael, they are two very different characters and personalities, but Jenson has the potential to become a winner. He is a good driver, and good drivers never give up.

Flavio Briatore, team chief, Benetton-Renault

I can definitely be a table thumper if that's what it takes, but I admit that it takes quite a lot to rile me. In Formula One everything has to be perfect, and when some things go wrong you do get angry because there's just so much at stake.

Ever since I arrived in Formula One my life off the track has changed. All the toys, the money and the media attention have attracted attention, but to my critics I would just say, yes, I have a lot of things, and I'm lucky to have them in some ways, though in others I think I deserve them because of what I do and the way in which I can do it. But there are still things in my life I'm not happy about. If you gave me a choice, swap all the toys you have for race wins in Formula One, I'd do it straight away. I need to win races. That's what I've always done for my whole life, since I was eight years old. It's what I'm used to. I won't be completely happy until I'm winning Formula One races, or at least in with a chance of winning. Then again, just because I can't do that at this stage of my career, I'm not going to hide away in a sulk. Life is there to enjoy, so I'm going to get on with it.

Away from racing I'm a pretty placid sort of bloke, although I don't get that sense of calm from religion. I haven't been christened or anything, and it's just not something I even think about. Of course I have shortcomings as a person, and if there's one failing that really irritates people, it's that I get bored very easily. I've always been hyperactive, everything in my life has always been fast-moving. After Formula One everything seems boring, because driving on Grand Prix circuits is so quick and so exciting. It can be very difficult outside racing to find something that excites me as much. I like an adrenalin rush, which is why I like to do exciting things. When I'm not being hyperactive I like to sleep, or watch TV. After a race weekend it's always nice to do that. But the next day I can never think of anything to do. Never. Louise has a really hard job with me, because I just get bored so easily. She's suggested getting some dogs, which should be fun, and might take some of the edge off the boredom.

I'm into sports a lot these days. I'm trying to play tennis. I hated sports when I was at school – apart, obviously, from karting. I actually didn't start to play tennis until towards the end of 2001, if you can believe that. Now Louise and I play a lot. But one reason I get bored so easily is that Louise is often away. She's quite busy a lot of the time and my friends are at uni when I'm at home. Formula One is such a strange lifestyle that you find yourself at home on days when other people are at work. I find it very difficult to occupy myself when I'm on my own. The funny thing is that I don't fraternize with any of the Formula One drivers who live in Monaco, although there are loads of them, but I'm sure we'll start getting together soon, maybe go out for rides into the mountains. Scare ourselves.

I hardly ever read books. I never read novels; I just find them dull. If I read anything, it'll be real-life stuff, not fiction. I read a book recently by Duncan Faulkner all about the Special Boat Service. I'm not about to have *Little Missy* converted into a gunship, I just read the book because of someone I know. I thought it would be a good read, and it was. It's probably the first book I've read all the way through for ages. I usually put them down about a third of the way in.

After Indy in 2001 Dad and I went to Maui for a short holiday before the Japanese Grand Prix. It was very relaxing, having nothing to do. We were in the south of the island, at the Hyatt Regency. I just went to the gym, sunned myself and did a bit of running in the morning and evenings. And I actually read another book there. I was going through the Tour de France winner Lance Armstrong's autobiography, *It's Not About the Bike*. That was quite sad because of what he's had to go through with cancer, but also uplifting because of the way he came back from that to be a winner again. He seems like a cool dude, and it's a mega book. I'm quite easily moved by those types of stories, especially when they take place in a sporting context because I can relate to some of the things the guy has gone through. It's so interesting to learn about what other sportsmen and women go through, the different ways in which they are affected by fitness, publicity, the press. Lance's autobiography is not just a book about a guy who had cancer and beat it; there are lots of other times when things have been very tough for him. It's good to see him win. I hadn't followed him closely before I read the book, but I have ever since.

When I really want to chill out – apart from the obvious, which gets me quite relaxed – I'll watch a vid or go to the cinema. When I'm at home I'm normally pretty relaxed. When I can't think of anything to do, I'll usually just train. Then in the evening I'll be tired, so I can just sit back without fidgeting in front of the TV, get a Chinese with Lou or one of my friends, maybe have the odd drink. I'm into red wine and beer. I normally drink the latter when I'm out with my friends, wine when I'm out with Lou. I do like champagne too, and I've got quite a bit of the stuff at the moment. It's a taste I've picked up since I got into Formula One. I haven't been boning up on Oz Clarke books or anything, I've just been in the fortunate position of being able to try lots of different types. There's one that I like a lot at the moment – it's called Louise. She loves champagne too. When her band releases its first album, I'm going to open a nice bottle to celebrate. I'm also quite partial to tequila with twelve shots of tabasco sauce. That's cool. I can recommend it. It's the new drink. I like apple juice too, especially with ice. And an umbrella!

My idea of a perfect night out is to eat at around eight, half eight, somewhere like Nobu, the Ivy or the Caprice in London, have a bottle of champagne and a nice meal (I like a good rump steak on nights like these, or a fillet steak, slightly pink on the inside), then go out to a couple of bars, meet up with some friends, go to a club, and basically have a fantastic time. I can't say whether or not I'm a good dancer because I'm usually too inhibited. I have to have a few inside me first. But when I do dance, I think it's awesome! I wouldn't say I'm good, though.

I celebrated my twenty-first birthday at Undercrofts, which is where I'd met Louise the previous year, and that was a great laugh. My birthday actually fell on a Friday, so I was able to scoot back from testing at Valencia in Spain. We had a Benetton-Renault on display, a giant Scalextric set and a cake shaped like a driver's helmet. We invited a whole load of family and friends and just chilled out. I'd really been looking forward to another chance to be with so many people who are special to me. There were people there from right back to my early days in racing, and others such as Colin Jackson, Jay Kay from Jamiroquai, Lou's mate Liz McClarnon from Atomic Kitten, James Cracknell and Beverley Turner. It was just a great evening.

It's nice to have money. I enjoy the things it buys, the lifestyle it allows you to lead. I like my boat, Little Missy. It's great for getting away from everything. Getting out to sea, doing loads of water-sports, skiing, whatever. I have jetskis and a rib boat that we can ski behind, and the big boat gets us out there so that we can enjoy these things. The summer of 2001 was fantastic. We were out all the time, out near Cannes. When my mates came out from Somerset we had the best week of our lives. It was fantastic. We just spent our time doing mad things, like jumping from the top of the boat. Normal bloke things. Being a little kid again. Really good fun. I think, though, that my best buy was an air-hockey table, which only cost me £500. Or a talking Winnie the Pooh, which has become my mascot.

I think about money a lot, but I definitely don't think I'm tight with it. I purposely try not to be. I try to help my family as much as possible in terms of finances. When it was time for me to look for a place of my own, I decided that I would make arrangements to move to Monaco. Prior to that I had arranged a house for my Dad in England. It was one way of saying thank you to him for everything he had done. This helped me to become an independent person. Louise and I enjoy being together in Monaco, so now everything is cool.

When Frank Williams told me how much he was going to pay for my services in 2000, naturally it felt terrific. The deal was very good and it was my first year in Formula One.

I love money – doesn't everybody? – but I'm certainly not motivated by it. Of course it's fantastic to have it, but most racing drivers wouldn't worry if they were paid less than they earn because of the sheer buzz of driving the cars. I want to race Formula One cars and I want to be the world champion, that's what motivates me. Those are the most important things to me as far as my career is concerned. But we have to spend so much time away from our homes, our families and friends, and we have to push the cars to the limit the whole time, right out on the edge, regardless of the dangers, that I think we deserve good money. As I said, though, I wouldn't have to have it. My job is fun, something I want to do, and I know a lot of people who would give their eye teeth to be able to do it. I feel very fortunate that my hobby is also my profession.

You meet some interesting people when you're a racing driver. I met Neve Campbell once at the *Scream II* première. She was quite a cool girl; I spent twenty minutes chatting her up. I've always liked her, as an actress of course, in *Scream* and her other movies. And I met Jamiroquai's Jay Kay at the British Grand Prix in 2000 when he wished me luck on the grid. He's a groovy guy. We get on well. I don't see him very often but we bump into each other every now and then. He's really into cars and racing. I'd like to see him more often, but he's busy with his albums and I'm busy with racing. But my life isn't quite as glamorous as it might seem because I don't get out much these days, with all the racing and testing. If I rub shoulders with celebrities, which everyone for some reason imagines I do all the time, it tends to be at the races. I hang out with my friends more, and tend not to go to the sort of places where celebrities go.

After DC won that British Grand Prix we all joined him for his party, where large amounts of vodka jelly and an ice machine were on offer. Ralf, Jacques and DC, Norbert Haug of Mercedes and I were all up on the stage. None of us could sing. It was quite funny because Dannii Minogue was there with Jacques as they were still together at that time, and he seemed to get a little bit embarrassed. I had a Rastafarian wig on. We were all hammered by eleven. Typical racing drivers – can't take a drop of drink.

I once did a duet with the late George Harrison in the back of a limo in Montreal. 'Yellow Submarine.' I honestly didn't know who he was. Of course I'd heard of him, and I knew the song, but I didn't know what he looked like. He was a top bloke. The world lost someone special when he succumbed to cancer in December 2001.

Then there was the time at Silverstone in April 2000 when Chris Evans kissed me on the lips. He came up to me after the race and I believe he said something like 'Fucking top bloke!' as he gave me a big wet smacker. Very odd. I can't say I enjoyed it very much, but life's full of experiences. But he's OK. I'd already done *TFI Friday* a couple of times with him, right at the start of my Formula One career. I got on well with him, he seemed quite cool. *TFI Friday* was fun, but it was pretty nerve-racking walking into the studio under the lights, waving to everyone. All the time you have a manic grin on your face and you're desperately hoping you won't trip over and make a complete fool of yourself.

When I got back to England in March 2000 after the Australian Grand Prix, Chris lent me his car, a Ferrari F550 Maranello (so he must be quite cool). I went out in it with my mate at Williams, Nav Sidhu. When we got to it, it was covered in dust and had a completely flat battery. We bump-started it from my BMW and then I drove it down the King's Road, parked it up somewhere, and later we had to bump-start it again. On a Ferrari you have to pull the handbrake up and it comes on; it then drops down but it's still on, so you have to pull it up a second time to release it. I didn't realize that at first, so I was driving down the King's Road thinking, 'Jesus, this thing is holding back a bit.' Right in the middle of the King's Road, where all these cars were at a junction, it just shuddered to a stop. It was dead on the ignition because the battery was still flat. So we just left it in the middle of the road with a dead battery and the handbrake jammed on and waited for the AA to come out. It was really embarrassing, all these people standing round taking pictures and saying, 'Jenson, well done! Hope you have a better race next weekend!' It even made the newspapers. Eventually we got it to Kwik-Fit for a new battery. A Kwik-Fit battery in a Ferrari! Then we had it for the rest of the day. Awesome! First time I'd ever driven a Ferrari like that.

People look at my lifestyle and think it's all champagne, fast cars, celebrities and designer suits. And yes, as I've admitted, I do like champagne. And I do buy expensive clothes, because I like them. But I've always done that. It's not just something that's developed after I came into Formula One. But I like other things too, and if they look good I buy them. I've bought jeans for twenty bucks, because I like them. I like expensive things, but the way they look is more the deciding factor than the price.

One way in which I tried to maintain a sense of perspective and keep my feet on the ground was to get involved with the National Blind Children's Society. I felt an affinity with it because it's based in Highbridge in Somerset, my home county, but my involvement goes a lot deeper than that. As racing drivers our eyes are so important to us. Of course sight is important to everyone, but acuity of vision is a fundamental requirement for all sportsmen. The NBCS offers specialized support to blind and partially sighted children and their families, and also aims to ensure that visually impaired children are given the best possible chance of independence in their adult lives. I feel privileged to be able to help them. The NBCS does great things for people who haven't got what we have. I hope that by becoming the society's vice-president I can help to raise awareness for the cause. A few of the kids came up to Silverstone when we were testing last year, and I've done some fundraising already. I'll be doing more this year, and I hope I can make some sort of contribution that will improve their lives, in whatever way. There's just something about children suffering that way. Many of them have been visually impaired since birth, and sight is something it's so very easy just to take for granted.

I have a great lifestyle, and of course I love being Jenson Button, Formula One driver. But then that's been my dream for half my life, so that shouldn't surprise anybody. It's all I've ever wanted to be. I don't worry what people think of me. It's what I think of myself that is important. And I'm happy with who I am.

SIXTEEN

THE ROAD AHEAD

As I've said, I'm not the sort to sit down and worry about everything. It's just not in my nature. Rather, I've found the coverage I received during my début season in Formula One and what was being written about me all the way through 2001 mildly amusing. I was the same guy, the same driver through 2000 and 2001. I was just in a different situation. But from being the Next Big Thing, Britain's next world champion, I was soon being written off either as a has-been – a has-been after one season, can you imagine that? – or somebody who'd just lucked in to some strong showings in my rookie season. People can think what they want, they've all got their own opinions and they're entitled to them, but I know what I'm capable of and that's what really matters.

I do read a fair bit of the stuff about me in newspapers and magazines, and some people have written critical pieces about me, but that's how they earn their living – writing stories that are interesting for their readers. If that means that they feel they have to be controversial or provocative, that's up to them. At various times during 2001 I was criticized by Sir Jackie Stewart, John Watson and Eddie Irvine, but to be honest I don't really take much notice of what Eddie says. I was amused by his reference to me as the 'Weakest Link', though. Very droll. A lot of people go through bad times and get criticized. It's part of the game, so I don't let it affect me. My first season with Benetton certainly wasn't the best, but I know 2002 will be better.

A lot of fuss was made over Kimi Raikkonen in his rookie season in 2001, and in many ways he went through what I did in 2000. I think he did an extremely good job, given that he had driven in just over twenty car races when he started testing for Sauber. I made history as the youngest driver ever to score a World Championship point; he made history as the first guy to jump to modern Formula One without even going through Formula Three. You have to say that's pretty cool. My former manager David Robertson, in partnership with his son Steve, manages Kimi, so at Monza a lot of people wanted to know why I didn't get the opportunity to go to McLaren for the 2002 season instead of Kimi. But Kimi did a great job in 2001 and deserves a good drive, and he was the one Ron Dennis asked about. People only look at your last performance in Formula One, which I don't think they should do so much. We'll see what Kimi can do up against DC in a big team like McLaren. I'm sure he'll go well, and I wish him luck.

During 2000 I gradually became accustomed to the media's ceaseless speculation about drivers' careers. I'd advise any aspiring Formula One racer to develop a thick skin. As early as the Spanish Grand Prix in April 2001 it all started again for me, when there were suggestions that my shoulder injury was so bad I was going to be 'rested' before Monaco. Then at the Nürburgring in June there were more rumours about my future in motorsport: I was going to be switched to Alain Prost's team, then it was Jaguar. Then, when it was announced that Kimi was moving to McLaren to replace Mika Hakkinen on his retirement, I heard that my contract was being offered to Sauber.

In any walk of life it gets unsettling when you hear so many rumours about what may or may not be happening to you, especially when such things are pretty much beyond your control. Formula One just isn't like real life: it's an insular world that to an extent subsists on all the gossip in the paddock. Everyone knows everyone else's business. Or they think they do. But just because they don't know for sure doesn't stop them speculating. In fact, that lack of inside knowledge is often what fuels the rumours. So you need a thick skin when things aren't going well. You need to roll with the punches. It's no good falling into the trap of believing the bad things people write about you any more than the good things that come your way. You just have to ignore it all and do your own thing. Most Formula One drivers are pretty self-confident people, and I'm no different in that respect. You need your complete focus on the job you're being paid well to do. Nothing else matters.

I'll be honest: in terms of being able to look forward positively, Hockenheim in July 2001 was a massive boost to my morale. No matter how resilient you are as a person – and I think I'm one of those pretty even-tempered people who don't let too much get on top of them – it is very hard to maintain maximum motivation when you go to a race knowing you not only have no chance of competing for points but are unlikely even to finish in the top ten. No matter how many times you tell yourself that you just have to be patient and bide your time waiting for the package to improve, you just want to be getting on with the job. It's not easy under such circumstances when the media is sniping at you because you're not matching your team-mate's performance. When things are tough –

and everyone and his dog knew in 2001 that things were very tough at Benetton – it becomes ever more important to beat him. When the car is not competitive enough for people to properly judge it, and you, against the opposition, your team-mate becomes an even more important barometer of your own performance. He is, after all, the only guy in the same boat as you. I certainly got plenty of flak whenever Giancarlo outqualified me.

I might have appeared to accept all that, but I was working my balls off trying to improve things. It was nice that people such as Pat Symonds and Patrick Head were saying good things in my defence around this time, and although it wasn't getting me down it was irksome that people seemed to take such a simplistic view of things. There's one thing you can be sure of in Formula One: nothing is simplistic! But the more you're tempted to try to explain things, the more some people take it as making excuses. Or, worse still, whingeing. Something I believe I have never been is a whinger!

I don't know what was happening at Benetton, I don't know whether Jenson got the second grade engine and aero bits. I'm not privy to all that. But I just get the impression that he's being raped by Formula One, if you want, by the glitz of it, the glamour, and by being signed up and having a rather grotty car. Or one that at least was not as competitive as the Williams. And he rather lost his way. I don't know his private life, whatever, it's none of my concern. But that will have an effect on a young guy who's doing his best. I think he needs to be in the right environment. I think the world of him. I think he's an absolute superstar. He just needed to get his frame of mind round the whole car and be strong. I don't know what they were doing with him at Benetton, but it must have been very difficult for him with a car that wasn't

exactly very good and engines that were going pop all the time. My heart felt for him, but at least things improved dramatically towards the end of the season.

What I saw that day with Prost in Barcelona was enough to convince me that the guy has got it. Look at how quick he was early on testing for Williams in Jerez, too. If a guy can learn circuits that quick it's one hell of a bonus in itself. You've just got to nurture him and point him in the right direction and feed all that talent. He needs good direction to concentrate totally on his racing, to get the best out of him. He's just a natural. Totally gifted. And he probably doesn't even realize it. Not too many people can do what he does. He just gets straight on it. I'm one of his biggest fans, and I hope he makes it.

Humphrey Corbett, Prost race engineer

Even before the race at Hockenheim I was feeling good, because though events didn't necessarily reflect it I should have out-qualified Giancarlo in France (and Germany itself) as I did in Britain, and would also have outraced him too, but for circumstances. My qualifying times and race times were competitive with his, so figuratively and literally I felt I was beginning to turn the corner.

I like Giancarlo. We're not the best of friends, because it's difficult to be bosom buddies with the guy you most need to beat, but I don't see any reason why you shouldn't get by on a human level. I'm not one of these people who gets secretive about set-up and technical matters. I'm just not made that way, and I wasn't brought up to be devious. I think the Buttons are a pretty open family! We say what we think, though I don't think any of us does that in a spiteful or thoughtless way. In any case, it doesn't help the team to progress when one driver tries to safeguard any secrets. Luckily, Giancarlo wasn't that way either.

Once we worked out how to make his set-up work on my car my pace picked up dramatically and things began to click. Some people think that copying a team-mate's set-up is a cop-out, that you should figure out yourself the way the car works best for you, but I've never had any problem using a different set-up if it makes me quicker. That's the name of the game! There were times in 2000 when I used Ralf's settings, and at other times he used mine. It is after all one reason why teams evolved into two-car set-ups – you get two cracks at it, and that's healthy.

At the British Grand Prix in July Giancarlo told the media that he expected our inter-team battle would be much closer for the rest of the season, which was decent of him. 'I'm a bit surprised at Jenson's pace,' he said, 'because for me he is a very quick driver. But he needs more experience. The car is not good, so my job is just to be quicker than my team-mate. But I've done eighty-three races and he's done only twenty-seven.' He didn't need to say that, even though he was right! To be honest, I would think he must be feeling as sick as a pig to be leaving Benetton now.

Jenson has a fundamental talent of being very solid and gifted. He is still on course to be a great driver after the Michael Schumacher era. I promise you that. He had a hard time in 2001, but it's easy to forget how complicated the modern Formula One cars are. You have to know what to do to get the best from them, and what not to do. Jenson is still young and relatively inexperienced. He doesn't know all the tricks. But last year he began to understand how tough it is and he began to apply his mind more and more to solving the problems. He needed time to catch up with Fisichella, who had been with

Benetton for some time. Jenson learned from his season and he got better as it progressed. He became a better, more capable driver because of that experience.

We want to win the World Championship again at Williams, and it would be very special if that happened with Jenson driving, after we effectively brought him into Formula One. I've always admired what Ron Dennis did with Mika Hakkinen when no-one would touch him in the early 1990s, when he was at the back of the grid and involved in so many accidents. Ron never gave up on Mika, and eventually he became a double world champion. All I'm saying is that we have an option on Jenson Button. Watch this space.

Frank Williams

By nature, I'm an optimistic sort of bloke. You just have to plug on through in hard situations. I knew I just had to keep on training, keep driving as hard as I could. I couldn't do much else, really. I just had to try to identify the problems and find ways around them. Some people don't do that. They just think things will magically get better. But if I have problems, I need to sort them. I can't see what hope you have in just taking a passive stance. So we worked very hard to locate those problems and nail them, and I think we did that. I hope, as Frank said, that I'm a better driver for all the problems. This year, we'll see. I worked hard in 2001, and as things progressed I think I found fresh directions for my efforts which were more fruitful. I think very hard about set-up; a difficult car forces you to look for a greater number of solutions. When a car is working well you just accept it and drive it hard; when a car isn't working so well you have to trawl through as many possible solutions as you can. I've learned a lot more about working on set-up, and I think my engineers are a lot happier for that as well.

Benetton definitely turned the corner at the back end of 2001; winter development suddenly held the promise of the ability to qualify in the top ten right from the start of the 2002 season, and then to push ever further forward.

How do I really feel about 2001? Well, bloody angry. What else would you expect me to feel? But it's over, and I'm only looking ahead now. I'm really pleased to be with Renault in 2002, because I'm convinced they've got their act together. It's a good team, and it's going to be a good place to be. We've laid down a lot of hard-won groundwork, and we're going to capitalize on that.

At the beginning of 2001 I told journalists that we were going to have a very tough time of it, and though some of them were sceptical, I was right. No surprises there. But I also said that I thought our performances would pick up in mid-season, and that we'd be strong by the end of the year. I was right about that too. A lot of people said to me, 'Wow, you made a lot of progress,' as if we'd done it overnight. Well, it was a load of nights. A lot of weekends. And it was gradual. But the fact is we made progress, which was gratifying. It meant that we were achieving our targets as a team and that all the elements – the design team, the engine men, the drivers, the tyre supplier – were doing their bit to move us forward. That's what makes me so confident that we will be in strong contention in 2002.

The other thing is that over the winter the guys in the design and construction departments had time to build the new car. They didn't have to rush into it the way they had to with the B201. Mike Gascoyne's input into the B201 wasn't anything like as big as everyone would have liked it to be because the model was broadly conceived before he was able to work out his contract with Jordan. That hasn't been the case with the new car, and he's working very well with our designers Tim Densham and Mark Smith.

All of them gel brilliantly, so I know they will give us a great car.

Renault itself is an amazing company. At Hockenheim we lost several engines on Friday and Saturday. Both Giancarlo and I had our qualifying engines in the cars on Saturday morning; his broke, then mine broke on my final run of the afternoon. The problem was an ongoing one: Renault Sport had been developing the engines continuously, so bits inside them were experimental and sometimes fragile. That also made it difficult for them to put specific engines into production. But that's how you make progress in Formula One. In James Hunt's days, Cosworth would introduce modifications to its DFV V8 engine at the beginning of the year and might then produce one major update part of the way through the season. But you can't do that today. Everyone is always developing something new. Things never stand still. Engine manufacturers constantly have to work on making their engines more powerful and more reliable, and of course the two things can be mutually incompatible at times. It's a very fine line to tread. Renault Sport had an even bigger problem because they took the gamble to introduce the revolutionary engine for 2001 to get the bugs out of it for 2002. It sounds trite to say it, because in Formula One anything other than a success story sounds like an excuse, such is the pressure of expectation, but we knew we would have a tough time with engines all through the season, so we had to take a philosophical stance and just wait for the good times to come. The fact that we both finished that race in Hockenheim, in fourth and fifth places, gave me enormous confidence in Renault's ability.

In the absence of the need to continue servicing engines because of the testing ban last November – instituted in order to give teams a break as well as to place some sort of limitation on spending – Renault were able to put a lot of extra effort into the 2002 engine. We have had the reliability to do a lot more testing with the new car prior to the start of the new season than we ever did last year, so being able to run a lot of kilometres right from the moment the car was ready has made a big difference. I'm not sure if we'll be winning races this year or fighting for the championship, but for sure we will be a lot closer than we were in 2001.

Unless you're in a team it's difficult to know the truth of any situation. I suspect that the car was so difficult at the beginning that there was the mental foot coming off the throttle, resigning himself to the fact that it was going to be a struggle and perhaps not applying himself. I think he had his problems with his engineers, which were resolved. He started off wrong there, but by the end of the year things were coming right and I'm sure they will continue to. He just needed to figure things out in his head and to work at it to get through that period. At the end of the day, in Formula One you've got to push hard all the time. There's no environment that is more competitive. But he did get through it. Look at his performances in the second half of the year.

Having said that, I think anyone who expected Jenson just to march straight into Benetton and turn the team round to his way of working was being naive. But he's really got to apply himself in 2002 because everyone will be watching him, including Frank and Patrick. And he will do, I'm quite sure. He's got talent. A bundle of it. People would be foolish to minimize or dismiss what he did with us in 2000. Given their vastly different levels of experience as they embarked on their first season of Formula One, I think what he did with us is not dissimilar to what Juan Pablo did in 2001.

Jim Wright, Head of Marketing, Williams F1 team

I trained like hell all through the winter. I needed to keep pro-
gressing on that front, and it's going to help me physically and
mentally. I needed to do some work on my back and upper body
because I had some back pains in the car last year, and proper training for that has really helped too.

Reluctantly, I also had to take some hard decisions about my
future, and at the end of 2001 I made revisions to my management
structure.

So I'm fit, I'm ready to go, and I'm really looking forward to
working with my new team-mate Jarno Trulli. Sure, we've had a
few brushes on the track – I think it's 2–1 against me at the
moment – but we've talked them through and everything's cool.
Neither of us is really keeping score. Jarno's a nice fellow and we've
known each other since our karting days. When I first came into
Formula One he said some welcoming things to me, which was a
good index of his character. I'm sure that, just as it happened with
Giancarlo, we will work strongly together. It's going to be a tough
battle between us, but we're both looking forward to that because
it will help to keep things on the boil and push the team forward.

It's funny, because we have this Ayrton Senna comparison thing
in common. When Jarno came into Formula One everyone kept
writing how much he looked like Ayrton around the eyes,
especially when he was wearing his crash helmet. Before I came in
I got saddled with a bit of an albatross round my neck, even though
my old karting entrant and mate Paul Lemmens's observation about
the best drivers he'd ever seen was meant in the best way. Now that
sort of thing is immensely flattering, given the driver that Ayrton
was, what he achieved and the affection and respect in which he
will always be held. But you can see why it can be embarrassing for
a young driver to wear such a tag. If you're not careful people start
to believe that's what you think yourself.

Jarno Trulli just wants to be Jarno Trulli, and I just want to be Jenson Button, hopefully in the same class as Ayrton Senna was. I'm not the youngest guy ever to have come into Formula One, but I was the youngest winner of the European Super A Karting Championship and I'd like to be the youngest ever Formula One world champion.

Believe me, I'm working on it.

INDEX

ACKNOWLEDGEMENTS

Writing a book is a bit like making a Grand Prix car – there's a lot more work goes into it than meets the eye. It's been quite an education for me to see how it's done, and there are a lot of people whom I have to thank for their significant roles in the story so far.

I could not have created this book without the outstanding assistance and efforts of freelance Formula One writer David Tremayne, who worked long hours to turn all our taped interviews into something highly readable. His professionalism and persistence are evident throughout. Martin Brundle once said that DT is like a stick of rock: with people he believes in he has loyalty stamped all the way through. I'm beginning to see what Martin means. He penned the story in the *Independent on Sunday* that predicted my success in the BRDC McLaren Autosport Young Driver Award in 1998, and remains an enthusiastic yet objective supporter.

We both had the backing of a great team at Transworld Publishers, whose professionalism has in turn formed our mutual efforts into a book we can both be proud of.

For their help in generating opportunities for me to further my career and/or in writing this book, I also owe my gratitude to: Sir Frank Williams, Patrick Head, Tim Preston, Jonathan Williams, Jim Wright and everyone at BMW Williams; Dr Mario Thiessen, Gerhard Berger and the crew at BMW Motorsport; Flavio Briatore, Mike Gascoyne, Pat Symonds, Paul Monaghan, Rod Nelson and all the guys at Renault Sport in Enstone; Hogne Rorvik, my physio, and my trainers Bernie Shrosbee and Phil Young; Jean-Jacques His and his team at Renault Sport in Viry-Chatillon; Fabiano and Lamberto Belletti at Team Rambo; Trevor Carlin of Carlin Motorsport; Humphrey Corbett; Bertrand Decoster and his team at Mygale; Neil Hann; Sue Holland; Tim Jackson at Renault UK; Paul Lambert; Paul, Lisette and Koen Lemmens and my mechanic Alex and the guys at GKS; Jude Martindale; Sergen Popovic; Alain Prost; Serge Saulnier at Promatecme; Joe Saward; Dave Spence; Russell Spence; John Surtees; Keith Sutton at Sutton Motorsport Images; Jim Warren, 'Puddy' Pullen and the team at Haywood Racing; John Village; Simon Wright at Wright Karts.

Most important of all are my family and friends. Mum and Dad had the great idea of having me in the first place and have always been my most ardent supporters. I owe so much of my racing career to Dad, who bought me my first kart and has been there alongside me ever since. His enthusiasm and faith have never wavered. You cannot buy that sort of support at any price.

My sisters Natasha, Samantha and Tanya and their families are always there for me too, while Louise Griffiths has become my rock and my helpmate. Believe me, I needed support from all of them in the dark times in 2001.

Finally, there are my friends, good mates that I have known since my schooldays who keep me firmly grounded. My thanks to them all.